SHOPPING AND FUCKING

Mark Ravenhill

**The Royal Court Writers Series published by
Methuen Drama in association with
the Royal Court Theatre and Out of Joint**

Royal Court Writers Series

First published in Great Britain in the
Royal Court Writers Series in 1996
by Methuen Drama
an imprint of Reed International Books Ltd
Michelin House, 81 Fulham Road, London SW3 6RB
and Auckland, Melbourne, Singapore and Toronto
in association with the Royal Court Theatre
Sloane Square, London SW1N 8AS
and distributed in the United States of America
by Heinemann, a division of Reed Elsevier Inc
361 Hanover Street, Portsmouth, New Hampshire 03901 3959

ISBN 0 413 71240 0

A CIP catalogue record for this book is available
at the British Library

Typeset by Country Setting, Woodchurch, Kent TN26 3TB
Printed in Great Britain by Cox & Wyman Ltd, Reading,
Berkshire

Out of Joint

Out of Joint is the acclaimed and award-winning theatre company established in 1993 by Max Stafford-Clark and Sonia Friedman to generate a substantial body of new writing for the stage, and to tour this work to theatres nationally and internationally. In some cases a classic play thematically linked to the new play is toured in tandem to encourage larger venues to make a fresh commitment to new writing.

Since 1994 the company has produced 14 tours, playing to over 300,000 people in over 50 theatres, nationally and internationally.

Out of Joint's inaugural production was the new play by Sue Townsend, **The Queen & I**, paired with Jim Cartwright's modern classic **Road**. After its extensive tour and run at the Royal Court, **The Queen & I** subsequently transferred to the West End. This summer a new Australian version of **The Queen & I** by Sue Townsend, entitled **The Royals Downunder** toured Australia. Out of Joint's second project was Stephen Jeffrey's new play **The Libertine** which toured in repertoire with the Restoration classic **The Man of Mode**. Next came the resounding success of the two Royal Court seasons and an international tour of **The Steward of Christendom** by Sebastian Barry. This was followed by a successful run at The Gate Theatre, Dublin. Following this Out of Joint produced **The Break of Day**, a new play by Timberlake Wertenbaker, which toured the U.K in repertoire with Chekhov's classic **Three Sisters**. Most recently **Three Sisters** toured India with the British Council, and then played in promenade at Rossway Park before its season at the Lyric Hammersmith.

In the immediate future Out of Joint is taking its original production of **The Steward of Christendom** to New York for a six-week season at BAM (the Brooklyn Academy of Music). Further ahead, in Spring 1997, plans include a co-production with the Hampstead Theatre of April de Angelis' new play **The Positive Hour**. In Autumn 1997 Out of Joint will premiere **Blue Heart**, two new one act plays by Caryl Churchill, in a co-production with The Royal Court Theatre, prior to a national and international tour.

After three years of touring new work Out of Joint has applied to The Arts Council of England for regular, fixed-term funding.

Artistic Director	Max Stafford-Clark
Producer	Sonia Friedman
Production & Company Manager	Rob Young
Literary Advisor	Philip Kingston
Administrative Assistant	Sally Pearson
Marketing	Mark Slaughter
Project Manager	Joanna Morgan
Press	Cameron Duncan Tel: 0171-383-0866

Katrina Levon and David Westhead in
The Libertine by Stephen Jeffreys.
Photo: Mark Douet

Out of Joint
20-24 Eden Grove
London N7 8ED
Tel 0171-609-0207
Fax 0171- 609-0203

Out of Joint is supported by the National Lottery through The Arts Council of England.

Out of Joint is also grateful to the following for their support over the past years: The Foundation for Sport and the Arts; The Paul Hamlyn Foundation; The Olivier Foundation; The Peggy Ramsay Foundation; The John S. Cohen Foundation; The David Cohen Foundation; The Baring Foundation; The Esmee Fairbairn Charitable Trust; Stephen Evans/Karl Sydow.

Stage Hands Appeal

Royal Court Theatre

The Royal Court (English Stage Company Ltd) has been given a once-in-a-lifetime opportunity to completely renovate and refurbish its facilities, at the Royal Court Theatre, Sloane Square, as a result of our £16 million National Lottery award.

However, as part of the terms of our award, the Royal Court must raise over £5 million in Partnership Funding towards the redevelopment.

This is obviously no small sum to raise, but rather than be daunted by all those zeros, the Royal Court has set a target of £500,000 in public donations, as just one element of our bid to bring this beautiful and important theatre up to date. Early fundraising from the public has already raised over £150,000 towards that target, which is a great start, so a huge thank you to all those who have contributed so far.

To help us continue our success we are now launching **Stage Hands** which is the umbrella name for all our public fundraising activities during the redevelopment. So if we're holding a benefit performance, a sponsored walk or a celebrity auction, these events will be part of our **Stage Hands** appeal.

We're now *handing* you a challenge; buy your **Stage Hands** T-shirt when you come to see *Shopping and Fucking* and wear it to our re-opening party at the Royal Court Theatre, Sloane Square in the Autumn of 1998.

For further details about **Stage Hands** or Partnership Funding please call Jacqueline Simons, Development Manager, on 0171-930-4253.

How the Royal Court is brought to you

The Royal Court (English Stage Company Ltd) is supported financially by a wide range of public bodies and private companies, as well as its own trading activities. The company receives its principal funding from the **Arts Council of England**, which has supported the Royal Court since 1956. The **Royal Borough of Kensington & Chelsea** gives an annual grant to the Royal Court Young People's Theatre and provides some of its staff. The **London Boroughs Grants Committee** contributes to the cost of productions in the Theatre Upstairs.

Other parts of the company's activities are made possible by business sponsorships. Several of these sponsors have made a long-term commitment. 1996 saw the sixth Barclays New Stages Festival of Independent Theatre, supported throughout by **Barclays Bank**. **British Gas North Thames** supported three years of the Royal Court's Education Programme. Sponsorship by **WH Smith** helped to make the launch of the Friends of the Royal Court scheme so successful.

1993 saw the start of our association with the **Audrey Skirball-Kenis Theatre**, of Los Angeles, which is funding a Playwrights Programme at the Royal Court. Exchange visits for writers between Britain and the USA complement the greatly increased programme of readings and workshops which have fortified the company's capability to develop new plays.

In 1988 the **Olivier Building Appeal** was launched, to raise funds to begin the task of restoring, repairing and improving the Royal Court Theatre, Sloane Square. This was made possible by a large number of generous supporters and significant contributions from the **Theatres Restoration Fund**, the **Rayne Foundation**, the **Foundation for Sport and the Arts** and the **Arts Councils Incentive Funding Scheme**.

The Company earns the rest of the money it needs to operate from the Box Office, from other trading and from the transfers of plays such as **Death and the Maiden**, **Six Degrees of Separation**, **Oleanna** and **My Night With Reg** to the West End. But without public subsidy it would close immediately and its unique place in British Theatre would be lost. If you care about the future of arts in this country, please write to your MP and say so.

The English Stage Company at the Royal Court Theatre

The English Stage Company was formed to bring serious writing back to the stage. The first Artistic Director, George Devine, wanted to create a vital and popular theatre. He encouraged new writing that explored subjects drawn from contemporary life as well as pursuing European plays and forgotten classics. When John Osborne's **Look Back in Anger** was first produced in 1956, it forced British Theatre into the modern age. But the Court was much more than a home for *'Angry Young Men'* illustrated by a repertoire that ranged from Brecht to Ionesco, by way of J P Sartre, Marguerite Duras, Wedekind and Beckett.

The ambition was to discover new work which was challenging, innovative and also of the highest quality, underpinned by the desire to discover a truly contemporary style of presentation. Early Court writers included Arnold Wesker, John Arden, David Storey, Ann Jellicoe, N F Simpson and Edward Bond. They were followed by a generation of writers led by David Hare and Howard Brenton, and in more recent years, celebrated house writers have included Caryl Churchill, Timberlake Wertenbaker, Robert Holman and Jim Cartwright. Many of their plays are now regarded as modern classics.

Since 1994 the Theatre Upstairs has programmed a major season of plays by writers new to the Royal Court, many of them first plays, produced in association with the *Royal National Theatre Studio* with sponsorship from *The Jerwood Foundation*. The writers included Joe Penhall, Nick Grosso, Judy Upton, Sarah Kane, Michael Wynne, Judith Johnson, James Stock and Simon Block.

Many established playwrights had their early plays produced in the Theatre Upstairs including Anne Devlin, Andrea Dunbar, Sarah Daniels, Jim Cartwright, Clare McIntyre, Winsome Pinnock, and more recently Martin Crimp and Phyllis Nagy.

Theatre Upstairs productions have regularly transferred to the Theatre Downstairs, as with Ariel Dorfman's **Death and the Maiden**, and last autumn Sebastian Barry's **The Steward of Christendom**, a co-production with *Out of Joint*.

1992-1995 have been record-breaking years at the box-office with capacity houses for productions of **Faith Healer**, **Death and the Maiden**, **Six Degrees of Separation**, **King Lear**, **Oleanna**, **Hysteria**, **Cavalcaders**, **The Kitchen**, **The Queen & I**, **The Libertine**, **Simpatico**, **Mojo** and **The Steward of Christendom**.

Death and the Maiden and **Six Degrees of Separation** won the Olivier Award for Best Play in 1992 and 1993 respectively. **Hysteria** won the 1994 Olivier Award for Best Comedy, and also the Writers' Guild Award for Best West End Play. **My Night with Reg** won the 1994 Writers' Guild Award for Best Fringe Play, the Evening Standard Award for Best Comedy, and Best Comedy 1994 Olivier Awards. Jonathan Harvey won the 1994 Evening Standard Drama Award for Most Promising Playwright, for **Babies**. Sebastian Barry won the 1995 Writers' Guild Award for Best Fringe Play for **The Steward of Christendom** and also the 1995 Lloyds Private Banking Playwright of the Year Award. Jez Butterworth won the 1995 George Devine Award for Most Promising Playwright, was named New Writer of the Year for by the Writers' Guild and won the Evening Standard Award for Most Promising Newcomer 1995 for **Mojo** and the 1995 Olivier Award for Best Comedy. Phyllis Nagy won the 1995 Writers' Guild Award for Best Regional Play for **Disappeared**. Martin McDonagh won the 1996 George Devine Award for Most Promising Playwright for **The Beauty Queen of Leenane**. The Royal Court was the overall winner of the 1995 Prudential Award for the Arts for creativity, excellence, innovation and accessibility, and the 1995 Peter Brook Empty Space Award for innovation and excellence in theatre.

Now in its temporary homes The Duke Of York's and Ambassadors Theatres, during the two year long refurbishment of the its Sloane Square base, the Royal Court continues to present the best in new work - after four decades the company's aims remain consistent with those established by George Devine. The Royal Court is still a major focus in the country for the production of new work. Scores of plays first seen at the Royal Court are now part of the national and international dramatic repertoire.

Society, Violence and the Theatre

"There are more scholars bred than the state can prefer and employ. It must need fall out that many persons will be bred unfit for other vocations which fill the realm full of indigent, idle and wanton people"
Francis Bacon 1611

"What? Because we are poor
Shall we be vicious?"
John Webster The White Devil 1612

"Unless we can use the theatre as a platform on which to demonstrate the serious problems of today, particularly violence, we feel that we are not serving a useful purpose in society"
Kenneth Tynan The Sunday Times July 1965

" Art isn't about itself. A writer has to tell the truth about society"
Edward Bond The Observer July 1976

Wallace Shawn: *The playwrights of my generation have a very strong sense that the society we live in is insane, that there is something very, very wrong...I meet people all the time over here in England who have such clearly defined views about society and the world that they actually know what they're going to think about things before they've even encountered them.*
Interviewer: *You don't have belief in other words.*
Wallace Shawn: *Well, we reserve the right to judge each new situation as it comes along...our frenzied glimpses of little worlds may be the best we can do*
Wallace Shawn: Fragment of An Interview November 1985

"When I read SAVED, I was deeply shocked by the baby being stoned. But then I thought... if you are saying you can't represent something, then...you are denying its existence, and that's an extraordinarily ignorant thing to do."
Sarah Kane The Times January 1995

"They will allow that the theatre may make people laugh, cry, be thrilled, entertained or ennobled, and to this last experience they allocate the role of tragedy. They are aided and abetted in this conviction by the sanctifying cloak of antiquity, poetry and all the moral eiderdowns that soften the edges and lend enchantment to the view. But to ennoble was not the original purpose of tragedy...its usefulness lay in its power as a cathartic, a jolly good belt in the stomach, purification through shock..."
Sir Laurence Olivier The Times November 1966

"The continuing power of this century's old monosyllable is gratifying. Its shock value has not disappeared...The F word still strikes many people with the crack of a rifle shot. There is still no consensus about its printability. The Times favours the f*** formula"
Brenda Maddox The Times August 1996

Shopping and Fucking

by Mark Ravenhill

Cast *in alphabetical order*

Lulu	Kate Ashfield
Robbie	Andrew Clover
Mark	James Kennedy
Gary	Antony Ryding
Brian	Robin Soans

Director	Max Stafford-Clark
Designer	Julian McGowan
Lighting Designer	Johanna Town
Sound Designer	Paul Arditti
Company Stage Manager	Rob Young
Deputy Stage Manager	Nick Marchand
Assistant Stage Manager	Lesley Huckstepp
Tour Electrician	Mark Doubleday
Assistant Director	Guy Retallack
Production Manager	Paul Handley
Production Photographer	John Haynes

With special thanks to the Royal National Theatre Studio who funded a workshop for *Shopping and Fucking* in June 1996.
The play was initially developed by work at the Finborough Theatre, London.

The Royal Court Theatre and Out of Joint would like to thank the following for their help with this production: Wardrobe care by Persil and Comfort courtesy of Lever Brothers Ltd, refrigerators by Electrolux and Philips Major Appliances Ltd.; kettles for rehearsals by Morphy Richards; video for casting purposes by Hitachi; backstage coffee machine by West 9; furniture by Knoll International; freezer for backstage use supplied by Zanussi Ltd 'Now that's a good idea.' Hair styling by Carole at Moreno, 2 Holbein Place, Sloane Square 0171 730 0211; Closed circuit TV cameras and monitors by Mitsubishi UK Ltd. Natural spring water from Wye Spring Water, 149 Sloane Street, London SW1, tel. 0171-730 6977. Overhead projector from W.H. Smith; Sanyo U.K for the backstage microwave.

Mark Ravenhill (writer)
Shopping and Fucking is Mark's first play.

Paul Arditti (sound designer)
For the Royal Court work includes: The Lights, The Thickness of Skin, Sweetheart, Bruises, Pale Horse, The Changing Room, Hysteria, Rat in the Skull (Royal Court Classics), Mojo, Simpatico, The Strip, The Knocky, Blasted, Peaches, Some Voices, Thyestes, My Night with Reg, The Kitchen, Live Like Pigs, Search and Destroy.
For the Royal Court-Out of Joint: The Steward of Christendom.
Other theatre sound design includes: As You Like It (RSC); Tartuffe (Manchester Royal Exchange) The Threepenny Opera (Donmar Warehouse); Hamlet (Gielgud); Piaf (Piccadilly); St. Joan (Strand & Sydney Opera House); The Winter's Tale, Cymbeline, The Tempest, Antony & Cleopatra, The Trackers of Oxyrhynchus (Royal National Theatre); The Gift of the Gorgon (RSC & Wyndhams);Orpheus Descending (Theatre Royal, Haymarket & Broadway); The Merchant of Venice (Phoenix & Broadway); A Streetcar Named Desire (Bristol Old Vic); The Winter's Tale (Manchester Royal Exchange); The Wild Duck (Phoenix); Henry IV, The Ride Down Mount Morgan (Wyndhams); Born Again, Fortune's Fool (Chichester); Three Sisters, Matador (Queens); Twelfth Night, The Rose Tattoo (Playhouse); Two Gentlemen of Verona, Becket, Cyrano de Bergerac (Theatre Royal, Haymarket); Travesties (Savoy); Four Baboons Adoring the Sun (Lincoln Center, 1992 Drama Desk Award).
Opera includes: Gawain, Arianna (ROH); The Death of Moses (Royal Albert Hall).

TV includes: The Camomile Lawn.

Kate Ashfield
For the Royal Court: Blasted, Peaches.
For Out of Joint-Royal Court: The Break of Day, Three Sisters
Other theatre includes: The Importance Of Being Earnest (Royal Exchange); A Collier's Friday Night, Bearing Fruit (Hampstead).
Television includes: Prime Suspect, Fist Of Fun, All Or Nothing, No Bananas, Soldier Soldier.
Film: Princess Caraboo.

Andrew Clover
Theatre includes: Jeffrey (Greenwich); Another Country (Man in the Moon).
Television includes: Cardiac Arrest, Aristophanes, The Bill.
Film includes: Marie Bes des Anges, True Blue, Love Waits, Joseph, Decadence.

James Kennedy
For the Royal Court; Thyestes, Pig in a Poke, Happy Days.
Other theatre includes: Something About Us (Lyric Studio); Marisol, Great Expectations (Traverse); The Master Builder (Riverside Studios): The Destiny of Me (Leicester Haymarket); Dr. Faustus. Mary Queen of Scots Got Her Head Chopped Off (Contact); Weights and Measures, Savage Britannia (RNT Studio); Macbeth, The Crucible, (Glasgow Citizens); The Comedy of Errors (Bristol Old Vic); The Public (Stratford East); The Alchemist (Cambridge Theatre Co.); Dr. Faustus, Philadelphia Here I Come (The Tron); Mumbo Jumbo (Lyric Hammersmith).
Television includes: Arise and Go Now, Parole, Prime Suspect III, Winners and Losers, The Houseman's Tale, The Bill.

Julian McGowan (designer)
For the Royal Court: Blood, American Bagpipes, Women Laughing (& Royal Exchange), The Treatment.
For Out of Joint - Royal Court: The Steward of Christendom, The Break of Day, Three Sisters.
Other theatre designs include: Translations (Abbey Theatre, Dublin); Old Times (Wyndhams, Theatr Clwyd); Venice Preserv'd,The Possibilities,The LA Plays (Almeida); Don Juan, The Lodger (Manchester Royal Exchange); Making History (set only/RNT); Heart Throb (Bush); Princess Ivona (ATC); Surgeon of Honour (Cheek by Jowl); Prin (Lyric, Hammersmith & West End); Leonce and Lena (Sheffield Crucible); The Tempest, Romeo and Juliet, Pericles, The Comedy of Errors (Oxford Stage Company); The Rivals, Man and Superman, Playboy of the Western World, Hedda Gabler (Glasgow Citizens); Imagine Drowning, Punchbag (Hampstead); Caesar & Cleopatra, Total Eclipse (Greenwich); Tess of the Durbervilles (West Yorkshire Playhouse); The Changeling (set only/RSC); The Lodger (Royal Exchange & Hampstead); Abigails Party, A Dolls House (Theatr Clwyd); The Wives Excuse (RSC); Torquatto Tasso (Edinburgh Festival); Playing the Wife, Simply Disconnected (Chichester Festival Theatre).
Opera includes: Cosi fan tutte (New Israeli Opera); Eugene Onegin (Scottish Opera); Siren Song (Almeida Opera Festival).

Guy Retallack
(assistant director)
For Out of Joint - Royal Court: The Break of Day,Three Sisters.
Other theatre includes: An Inspector Calls, The Wind in the Willows (RNT/PW Productions); The Queen and I (tour); For a

Company of Clerks, Ivan Vasilievich (BAC Studio 1); The Millionairess, The Master and Margarita (BAC Mainhouse); The New Apartment (Watermans Arts); The Basset Table (New End); Bligh (ETC).
As assistant director: The Liar, Marta (Old Vic); Grand Magic (Assembly Rooms); All My Sons, Romeo and Juliet (Oxford Stage Company).

Antony Ryding

Theatre includes: What I Did In the Holidays (Cambridge Theatre Company); Strung Bead, The Graiae (Trading Faces); She'll Be Coming Round the Mountain (Backstairs Influence).

Robin Soans

For the Royal Court: Waiting Room Germany, Star-Gazy Pie and Sauerkraut, Three Birds Alighting on a Field (1991 & 1992), Etta Jenks, Bed of Roses (also Bush & tour).
Other theatre includes: Volpone (RNT); Raising Fires (Bush); The Country Wife, The Venetian Twins, Murder in the Cathedral (RSC); Walpurgis Night, Gringo Planet (Gate); Germinal, Berlin Days - Hollywood Nights (The Place & tour); Bet Noir (Young Vic);Fashion(Leicester Haymarket&Tricycle); Thatcher's Women (Tricycle & tour); The Rivals (Nottingham Playhouse); A Prick Song for the New Leviathan (Old Red Lion); The Shaming of Bright Millar (Contact Manchester); Queer Fish (BAC); The Worlds, Hamlet,Woyzec, Chobham Amour (Half Moon); The Strongest Man in the World (Round House).
Television includes: Casualty, The Marshall and the Madwoman, Inspector Alleyn, Anna Lee, Lovejoy, The Specials, This Land of England, The Last Place on Earth, The Chelworth

Inheritance, Bergerac, Lord Peter Wimsey, The Bill, Tales of Sherwood Forest, Bard on the Box.
Films include: Comrades, Absolution, The Patricia Neal Story, Hidden City, Blue Juice, Clockwork Mice.

Max Stafford-Clark

(director)
Studied at Trinity College, Dublin.
Following his Artistic Directorship of The Traverse Theatre, Edinburgh, Max Stafford-Clark founded Joint Stock Theatre group in 1974. From 1979 to 1993 he was Artistic Director of The Royal Court Theatre. In 1993 he founded his touring company Out of Joint, and he is also an Associate Director of The Royal Court Theatre. His work as a Director has overwhelmingly been with new writing, and he has commissioned and directed many first productions. These include: *Fanshen, The Speakers* (both with WilliamGaskill), *Light Shining in Buckinghamshire* and *Cloud Nine* for Joint Stock; *The Arbor, Operation Bad Apple, Top Girls, Rita Sue and Bob Too, Falkland Sound, Tom and Viv, Rat in the Skull, Aunt Dan and Lemon, Serious Money, Our Country's Good, Icecream, My Heart's a Suitcase, Hush* and *Three Birds Alighting on a Field* for the Royal Court; *The Queen And I, The Libertine, The Steward of Christendom* and *The Break of Day* for Out of Joint.
In addition he has directed *The Seagull, The Pope's Wedding,. The Recruiting Officer* and *King Lear* for the Royal Court; *A Jovial Crew, The Country Wife* and *The Wives Excuse* for the RSC; *The Man of Mode* and *Three Sisters* for Out of Joint.

He has also directed for The Abbey Theatre, Dublin and Joseph Papp's Public Theatre, New York.
His book *Letters to George* was published in 1989.

Johanna Town

(lighting designer)
For the Royal Court: Harry and Me, The Kitchen, Faith Healer, Babies, The Editing Process, Pale Horse, Peaches, Search & Destroy, Women Laughing, Talking in Tongues.
For Out of Joint - Royal Court: The Steward of Christendom, Three Sisters, Road, The Break of Day.
Other theatre lighting designs include: Beautiful Thing (Duke of York's Theatre, Donmar, Bush); Charley's Aunt (Watford, Southampton); The Lodger (Royal Exchange Theatre, Hampstead); Richard II, Street Captives, The Misfits (Royal Exchange Theatre); Disappeared (Leicester Haymarket and tour); Salvation, The Snow Orchid (London Gay Theatre); The Set-Up, Crackwalker (Gate Theatre); Stiff Stuff (Library Theatre); Celestina (ATC): Josephine (BAC); Three seasons at the Liverpool Playhouse including: Macbeth, Madame Mao, Beaux Stratagem.
Opera credits includes: Otello (Opera du Nice);La Traviata, The Magic Flute, The Poisoned Chalice (M.T.L. Donmar, Hamburg, Holland); The Marriage of Figaro, Eugene Onegin, The Abduction from the Seraglio, (Opera 80); The Human Voice, Perfect Swine (MTM).
Currently Head of Lighting at the Royal Court.

JERWOOD
NEW PLAYWRIGHTS

Jerwood New Playwrights sees the Jerwood Foundation coming forward for a second year as a major sponsor of the Royal Court Theatre. This series of six plays staged in the winter and spring of 1996-7, will be a notable celebration of the best of contemporary playwriting. Certain of the plays have already reached the Royal Court stage last year, to great acclaim - **Mojo** by Jez Butterworth and **The Beauty Queen of Leenane** by Martin McDonagh. The fact that others are new plays underlines still further the notable importance of the Royal Court as a forcing ground for new talent.

I am a great admirer of the exceptionally high artistic level the Royal Court has achieved. This achievement fits perfectly with the ideals of the Jerwood Foundation, a private foundation established in 1977 by the late John Jerwood. It is dedicated to imaginative and responsible funding and sponsorship of the arts, education, design, conservation, medicine, science and engineering, and of other areas of human endeavour and excellence.

The Foundation is increasingly known for its support of the arts. In the field of the visual arts, two major awards are increasingly bringing it to public attention. The first is the Jerwood Painting Prize, now in its third year and the most valuable art prize in the United Kingdom. The second is the Jerwood Foundation Prize for Applied Arts, the largest prize of its kind in Europe, which in 1996 was offered for ceramics.

The Council of the Foundation has singled out one particular strand for development within the Foundation's varied field of benefactors: support of talented young people who have perservered in their chosen career and will benefit from the financial support and recognition which will launch them. To achieve this goal, a number of awards and sponsorships have been developed in concert with organisations such as the Royal Ballet Companies (for the Jerwood Young Choreographers Awards); the National Film and Television School; the Royal Academy of Dancing; and The Royal Academy of Engineering.

The Foundation sponsors the Brereton International Music Symposium which gives masterclasses for young professional windplayers and singers, the National Youth Chamber Orchestra, and the Opera and Music Theatre Lab at Blore Place in Kent. In 1996, with The Big Issue it co-sponsored The Big Screening , a free season of new films by British directors. Across all the arts, it is vital that financial support be given to the creation of new work. It is for this simple reason that we are delighted to be sponsoring another exciting season with the Royal Court.

Alan Grieve
Chairman

A Note on the Text

A quick word. If you are sitting in your seat at the Royal
Court Upstairs or the Liverpool Everyman or the Hawth
Crawley – or anywhere else that the first production of
my play *Shopping and Fucking* is playing – and, as the action
unfolds, you are tempted to follow the words in this
remarkably reasonably priced programme-playtext, may
I offer some advice? *Don't even try.*

And don't be too disappointed if you get this book home
only to find that your favourite (or least favourite) moment
from your evening out is nowhere to be found in these
pages. And if you are reading this text but never got a
chance to see the production – well, you probably missed
some really good bits.

As this text goes to print, we are less than half way
through a rehearsal process in which every word, every action
of my first play is being tested, worked on and reworked by
myself, the director Max Stafford-Clark and the cast. Who
knows what further discoveries and changes we will have
made by the time we share the play with an audience?

For some playwrights – me included – it is only in the
atmosphere of the rehearsal room that our characters,
scenes and ideas are fully clarified. Fired by the company's
persistent questions – what am I doing? how should I do
it? how will my decision impact on the play and its repre-
sentation of the world? – the text finds its final shape.

The theatre is a public medium and should, I think, do
more than invite audiences to witness the writer's private
world. With a perceptive director and fearless actors, such
as those I have been blessed with for *Shopping and Fucking,* a
collaborative way of working challenges a playwright to tap
into a vein of our common humanity.

So, please excuse the strange divergences between the
script in your hand and the play on the stage. Right now
I'm going back to the rehearsal room. There's been some
mention of an Ecstasy workshop and I feel it's absolutely
vital that the playwright takes part. Bliss to all.

Mark Ravenhill, September 1996

Scene One

Flat — once rather stylish, now almost entirely stripped bare.

Lulu *and* **Robbie** *are trying to get* **Mark** *to eat from a carton of take-away food.*

Lulu   Come on. Try some.

Pause.

Come on. You must eat.

Pause.

Look, please. It's delicious. Isn't that right?

Robbie   That's right.

Lulu   We've all got to eat.
Here.
Come on, come on.
A bit for me.

Mark *vomits.*

Robbie   Shit. Shit.

Lulu   Why does that alw . . . ?
Darling — could you? Let's clean this mess up.
Why does this happen?

Mark   Please.

Lulu   This will . . . come on . . . it's all right.

Mark   Look, please.

Lulu   Thank you.
See? It's going. Going . . . going . . . gone.

Robbie   All right? OK?

Lulu   Yes, yes. He's all right now.

Mark   Look . . . you two go to bed.

Lulu   Leave you like this?

Mark I want to be alone for a while.

Robbie Is someone coming round?

Lulu Do you owe money?

Mark No. No one's coming round. Now – go to bed.

Lulu So what are you going to do?

Mark Just sit here. Sit and think. My head's a mess. Look at me. I'm fucked.

Robbie You'll be all right.

Mark I'm so tired.
I can't control anything. My . . . guts. My mind.

Robbie We have good times, don't we?

Mark Of course we have. I'm not saying that.

Robbie Good times. The three of us. Parties. Falling into taxis, out of taxis. Bed.

Mark That was a long time ago.

Lulu Watching you on the floor. Us on the balcony. And your hands – tic, tac. Trading. All that money. And later – that wine bar – so high on it we couldn't wait. Three of us in the toilet and we came and came and came.

Mark It was years ago. That was the past.

Lulu That night you said: I love you both and I want to look after you for ever and ever.

Mark Look I . . .

Lulu Tell us the shopping story.

Mark Please, I want to . . .

Robbie Yeah, come on. You still remember the shopping story.

Pause.

Mark Well all right.
I'm watching you shopping.

Lulu   No. Start at the beginning.

Mark   That's where it starts.

Robbie   No it doesn't. It starts with: 'summer'.

Mark   Yes. OK.
It's summer. I'm in a supermarket. It's hot and I'm sweaty.
Damp. And I'm watching this couple shopping. I'm
watching you. And you're both smiling. You see me and
you know sort of straight away that I'm going to have you.
You know you don't have a choice. No control.
Now this guy comes up to me. He's a fat man. Fat and
hair and Lycra and he says:
'See the pair by the yoghurt?'
'Well,' says fat guy, 'they're both mine. I own them. I own
them but I don't want them – because, you know
something? – They're trash. Trash and I hate them. Wanna
buy them?'
'How much?'
'Piece of trash like them? Let's say . . . twenty. Yeah, yours
for twenty.'
So, I do the deal. I hand it over. And I fetch you. I don't
have to say anything because you know. You've seen the
transaction.
And I take you both away and I take you to my house.
And you see the house and when you see the house you
know it. You understand? You know this place.
And I've been keeping a room for you and I take you into
this room. And there's food. And it's warm. And we live
out our days fat and content and happy.

Pause.

Listen. I didn't want to say this. But I have to.

I'm going.

Lulu   Going out?

Robbie   You're going to score?

Lulu   Scag. Loves the scag.

Mark Not any more.

Robbie Loves the scag more than he loves us.

Mark Look. Look now. That isn't fair. I hate the scag.

Lulu Still buying the scag though, aren't you?

Mark No. I'm off the scag. Ten days without the scag. And I'm going away.

Robbie From us?

Mark Yes. Tonight.

Lulu Where are you going?

Mark I want to get myself sorted. I need help. Someone has to sort me out.

Robbie Don't do that. You don't need to do that. We're helping you.

Lulu We're sorting you out.

Mark It's not enough. I need something more than you.

Robbie You're going? And leaving us?

Mark I'm going to get help.

Robbie Haven't we tried? We've tried. What do you think we've been doing? All this time. With the . . . clearing up when you, you . . .

Lulu Where?

Mark Just a place.

Lulu Tell us.

Mark A centre. For treatment.

Lulu Are you coming back?

Mark Of course I am.

Robbie When?

Mark Well, that all depends on how well I respond. To the treatment. A few months.

Robbie   Where is it? We'll visit.

Mark   No.

Robbie   We'll come and see you.

Mark   I musn't see you.

Robbie   I thought you loved me. You don't love me.

Mark   Don't say that. That's a silly thing to say.

Lulu   Hey. Hey, look. If you're going, then go.

Robbie   You don't love me.

Lulu   Look what you've done. Look what you've done
to him.
What are you waiting for? A taxi? Maybe you want me to
call a taxi? Or maybe you haven't got the money? You
going to ask me for the money?
Or maybe just take the money? You've sold everything.
You've stolen.

Mark   Yes. It's not working. That's why I'm going.

Lulu   Yes. I think you should. No. Because we're going to
be fine. We're going to do very well. And I think maybe
you shouldn't come back. We won't want you back.

Mark   Let's wait and see.

Lulu   You don't own us. We exist. We're people. We can
get by. Go.
Fuck right off. Go. GO.

Mark   Goodbye.

Exit **Mark**.

Robbie   Don't go. I don't want you to go. Please. Stay.
I'll be good. I'll help you. You'll get better.

Lulu   He's gone now. Come on. He's gone.
We'll be all right. We don't need him. We'll get by. Come
on. SSssssssh. Sssshhh.

Scene Two

Interview room.

Brian *and* **Lulu** *sit facing each other.* **Brian** *is showing* **Lulu** *an illustrated plastic plate.*

Brian   And there's this moment. This really terrific moment. Quite possibly the best moment. Because really, you see, his father is dead. Yes? The father was crushed – you feel the sorrow welling up in you – crushed by a wild herd of these big cows. One moment, lord of all he surveys. And then . . . a breeze, a wind, the stamping of a hundred feet and he's gone. Only it wasn't an accident. Somebody had a plan. You see?

Lulu   Yes. I see.

Brian   Any questions. Any uncertainties. You just ask.

Lulu   Of course.

Brian   Because I want you to follow.

Lulu   Absolutely.

Brian   So then we're . . . there's . . .

Lulu   Crushed by a herd of wild cows.

Brian   Crushed by a herd of wild cows. Yes.

Lulu   Only it wasn't an accident.

Brian   Good. Excellent. Exactly. It wasn't an accident. It may have looked like an accident but – no. It was arranged by the uncle. Because –

Lulu   Because he wanted to be King all along.

Brian   Thought you said you hadn't seen it.

Lulu   I haven't.
Instinct. I have good instincts. That's one of my qualities. I'm an instinctive person.

Brian   Is that right?

Brian *writes down 'instinctive' on a pad.*

Brian   Good. Instinctive. Could be useful.

Lulu   Although of course I can also use my rational side. Where appropriate.

Brian   So you'd say you appreciate order?

Lulu   Order. Oh yes. Absolutely. Everything in its place.

Brian *writes down 'appreciates order'.*

Brian   Good. So now the father is dead. Murdered. It was the uncle. And the son has grown up. And you know – he looks like the dad. Just like him. And this sort of monkey thing comes to him. And this monkey says: 'It's time to speak to your dead dad.'   So he goes to the stream and he looks in and he sees –

Lulu   / His own reflection.

Brian   His own reflection. You've never seen this?

Lulu   Never.

Brian   But then . . . The water ripples, it hazes. Until he sees a ghost. A ghost or a memory looking up at him. His . . .

Pause.

Excuse me. It takes you right here. Your throat tightens. Until . . . he sees . . . his . . . dad.
My little one. Gets to that bit and I look round and he's got these big tears in his eyes. He feels it like I do.
Because now the dad speaks. And he says: 'The time has come. It is time for you to take your place in the Cycle of Being (words to that effect). You are my son and the one true King.'
And he knows what it is he's got to do. He knows who it is he has to kill.
And that's the moment. That's our favourite bit.

Lulu   I can see that. Yes.

Brian   Would you say you in any way resembled your father?

Lulu   No. Not really. Not much.

Brian   Your mother?

Lulu   Maybe. Sometimes. Yes.

Brian   You do know who your parents are?

Lulu   Of course. We still . . . you know. Christmas. We spend Christmas together. On the whole.

Brian *writes down 'celebrates Christmas'.*

Brian   So many today are lost. Isn't that so?

Lulu   I think that's right. Yes.

Brian   All they want is something.
And some come here. They look to me. You're looking to me aren't you?
Well aren't you?

Lulu   Yes. I'm looking to you.

Brian (*proffers plate*)   Here. Hold it. Just hold it up beside you. See if you look right. Smile. Look interested. Because this is special. You wouldn't want to part with this. Can you give me that look?

Lulu *attempts the look.*

Brian   That's good. Very good. Our viewers, they have to believe that what we hold up to them is special. For the right sum – life is easier, richer, more fulfilling. And you have to believe that too. Do you think you can do that?

Again **Lulu** *attempts the look.*

Brian   Good. That's very good. We don't get many in your league.

Lulu   Really?

Brian   No. That really is very . . . distinctive.

Lulu   Well. Thank you. Thanks.

Brian   And now: 'Just a few more left. So dial this number now.'

Lulu   Just a few more left. So dial this number now.

Brian   Excellent. Natural. Professional. Excellent.

Lulu   I have had training.

Brian   So you're . . . ?

Lulu   I'm a trained actor.

Brian *writes down 'trained actor'.*

Brian   I don't recognize you.

Lulu   No? Well, probably not.

Brian   Do some for me now.

Lulu   You want me to . . . ?

Brian   I want to see you doing some acting.

Lulu   I didn't realize. I haven't prepared.

Brian   Come on. You're an actress. You must be able to do some acting.
An actress – if she can't do acting when she's asked, then what is she really?
She's nothing.

Lulu   All right.

Lulu *stands up.*

Lulu   I haven't actually done this one before. In front of anyone.

Brian   Never mind. You're doing it now.

Lulu   One day people will know what all this was for. All this suffering.

Brian   Take your jacket off.

Lulu   I'm sorry?

Brian   I'm asking you to take your jacket off. Can't act with your jacket on.

Lulu   Actually, I find it helps.

Brian   In what way?

Lulu   The character.

Brian   Yes. But it's not helping me. I'm here to assess your talents and you're standing there acting in a jacket.

Lulu   I'd like to keep it on.

Brian (*stands*)   All right. I'll call the girl. Or maybe you remember the way?

Lulu   No.

Brian   What do you mean – no?

Lulu   I mean . . . please, I'd like this job. I want to be considered for this job.

Brian   Then we'll continue. Without the jacket. Yes?

Lulu *removes her jacket. Two chilled ready meals fall to the floor.*

Brian   Look at all this.

They both go to pick up the meals. **Brian** *gets there first.*

Brian   Exotic.

Lulu   We've got really into them. That's what we eat. For supper.

Brian   Did you pay for these?

Lulu   Yes.

Brian   Stuffed into your jacket. Did you pay for them?

Lulu   Yes.

Brian   Look me in the eyes. Did. You. Pay?

Lulu   No.

Brian Stolen goods.

Lulu We have to eat. We have to get by. I don't like this.
I'm not a shoplifter. By nature. My instinct is for work.
I need a job. Please.

Brian You're an actress by instinct but theft is a necessity.
Unless you can persuade me that I need you. All right.
Carry on. Act a bit more.
No shirt.

Lulu No . . .?

Brian Carry on without the . . . (what's the . . . ?) . . .
blouse.

Lulu *removes her blouse.*

Lulu One day people will know what all this was for. All
this suffering. There'll be no more mysteries. But until then
we must carry on working. We must work. That's all we
can do. I'm leaving by myself tomorrow . . .

Brian (*stifling a sob*) Oh, God.

Lulu I'm sorry. Shall I stop?

Brian Carry on. As you were.

Lulu Leaving by myself tomorrow. I'll teach in a school
and devote my whole life to people who need it. It's
autumn now. It will soon be winter and there'll be snow
everywhere. But I'll be working.
That's all.

Lulu *puts her shirt and jacket on.*

Brian (*wipes away a tear*) Perfect. Brilliant. Did you make
it up?

Lulu No. I learnt it. From a book.

Brian Brilliant. So you think you can sell?

Lulu I know I can sell.

Brian Because you're an actress?

Lulu   It helps.

Brian   You seem very confident.

Lulu   I am.

Brian   All right then. A trial. Something by way of a test. I'm going to give you something to sell and we're going to see how well you do. Clear so far?

Lulu   Totally.

Brian   You understand that I am *entrusting* you?

Lulu   I understand.

Brian   I am entrusting you to pass this important test.

Lulu   I'm not going to let you down.

Brian   Good.

Brian *reaches for his briefcase and starts to open it.*

Scene Three

Flat.

Robbie *is sitting. He is wearing the uniform of a leading burger chain.* **Lulu** *stands over him.*

Robbie   And I've said: 'With cheese, sir?'
And he just looks at me blankly. Just stares into my eyes.
And there's this . . . fear.
Try again. 'Would you like cheese on your burger sir?'
This is too much for him. I see the bottom lip go. The eyes are filling up.

Lulu   So you told him. And they sacked you?

Robbie   Someone had to. If you were there you'd . . .
I decide I'm going to have to tell him. And I say:
'Look, here you have a choice. For once in your life you have a choice so for fuck's sake make the most of it.'

Lulu   And then they sacked / you?

Robbie   And then. Then. He gets this fork. Grabs this fork. And he jumps over the counter. And he goes for me.

Lulu   With the fork?

Robbie   Goes for me with the fork. Gets me down and stabs me.

Lulu   He stabbed you?

Beat.

Robbie   It's nothing.

Lulu   You're wounded. You should have told me.

Robbie   No. It's nothing.

Lulu   Where's the wound then?

Robbie   It snapped. Before it did any damage.

Lulu   ?

Robbie   The fork. It was a plastic fork. It snapped before it did any damage.

Pause.

Lulu   So. Where's the money going to come from? Who's gonna pay for everything?

Robbie   You'll come up with something.

Lulu   Me?

Robbie   Yeah. You'll sort it out.
Did you get it?

Lulu   Did I get . . . ?

Robbie   The job. The TV.

Lulu   Well. Yes. They're taking me on . . .

Robbie   Brilliant. / That's brilliant.

Lulu   They're offering me a sort of temporary assignment.

Robbie   Yeah? What sort of . . . ?

Lulu *produces three hundred E in a clear bag.*

Robbie   You're gonna / sell them?

Lulu   We're going to sell them. You can make yourself useful.
Should be three hundred. You can count them.

Exit **Lulu**. **Robbie** *starts counting the tablets.* **Mark** *enters and watches* **Robbie**, *who doesn't see him until* –

Mark   Are you dealing?

Robbie   Fuck. You made me –
How long have you – ?

Mark   Just now. Are you dealing?

Robbie   That doesn't . . .

Pause.

So. They let you out.

Mark   Sort of.

Pause.

Robbie   Thought you said months. Did you miss me?

Mark   I missed you both.

Robbie   I missed you. So, I s'pose . . . I sort of hoped you'd miss me.

Mark   Yeah. Right.

Robbie *moves to* **Mark**. *They kiss.*
Robbie *moves to kiss* **Mark** *again.*

Mark   No.

Robbie   No?

Mark   Sorry.

Robbie   No. That's OK.

Mark   No, sorry. I mean it. Because actually I'd decided I wasn't going to do that. I didn't really want that to happen, you know? Commit myself so quickly to . . . intimacy.

Robbie   OK.

Mark   Just something I'm trying to work through.

Robbie   . . . Work through?

Mark   Yeah. Sort out. In my head.
We've been talking a lot about dependencies. Things you get dependent on.

Robbie   Smack.

Mark   Smack, yes absolutely. But also people. You get dependent on people. Like . . . emotional dependencies. Which are just as addictive, OK?

Robbie (*pause*)   So – that's it, is it?

Mark   No.

Robbie   That's me finished.

Mark   No.

Robbie   'Goodbye.'

Mark   I didn't say that. No. Not goodbye.

Robbie   Then . . . kiss me.

Mark   Look . . . (*Turns away.*)

Robbie   Fuck off.

Mark   Until I've worked this through.

Pause.

Robbie   Did you use?

Mark   No.

Robbie   Right. You used, they chucked you out.

Mark   Nothing. I'm clean.

Robbie   So . . . .?

Pause.

Mark   There are these rules, you see. They make you sign – you agree to this set of rules. One of which I broke. OK?

Robbie   Which one?

Mark   It was nothing.

Robbie   Come on.

Mark   I told them. It wasn't like that. I put my case / but

Robbie   *Tell me.*

Pause.

Mark   No personal relations.

Robbie   Fuck.

Mark   You're not supposed to – form an attachment.

Robbie   Ah, I see.

Mark   Which I didn't.

Robbie   So that's why / you won't kiss me.

Mark   It wasn't an attachment.

Robbie (*pause*)   If you were just honest. We said we'd be honest.

Mark   It wasn't like that. I told them 'You can't call this a personal relationship.'

Robbie   What was it then?

Mark   More of a . . . transaction. I paid him. I gave him money. And when you're paying, you can't call that a personal relationship, can you? / What would you call it?

Robbie   You can't kiss me. You fucked someone / but you can't kiss me.

Mark   That would mean something.

Robbie   Who was it?

Mark   Somebody.

Robbie   Tell me who.

Mark   He was called Wayne.

Robbie   Well . . . get you.

Mark   I just – you know – in the shower. Shower and I . . . Saw his bottom. Saw the hole, you know. And I felt like – I wanted to . . . lick it.

Robbie (*pause*)   That's it?

Mark   We did a deal. I paid him. We confined ourselves to the lavatory. It didn't mean anything.

Robbie   Nothing for afters?

Mark   That's all.

Robbie   Just Lick and Go.

Mark   It wasn't a personal relation.

Robbie (*lets trousers drop*)   Well, if you can't kiss my mouth.

Mark   No. With you – there's . . . baggage.

Robbie   Well, excuse me. I'll just have to grow out of it.

Robbie *pulls his trousers up. Pause.*

Mark   I'm sorry.

Robbie   Sorry? No. It's not . . . sorry doesn't work. Sorry's not good enough.

Pause.

Mark   You're dealing?

Robbie   Doesn't matter.

Mark   Thought so.

Robbie   Listen, this stuff is happiness. Little moment of heaven. And if I'm spreading a little – no a great big fuck-off load of happiness –

Pause. **Robbie** *picks up an E between thumb and forefinger.*

Mark   It's not real.

Robbie   Listen if you, if this, this . . . planet is real . . .

Robbie *takes an E. Pause.*

Waiting for you. Do you know what it's like – waiting? Looking forward to this day – for you to . . . And you – Oh, fuck it. Fuck it all.

Robbie *takes another E.*

Enter **Lulu** *with two microwaved ready meals on a tray.*

Lulu   I . . . They let you out. It's sooner . . .

Mark   Yeah. They let me out. Thought I'd come back. See if you're all right.

Pause.

Lulu   I've only got enough for two.

Mark   Never mind.

Lulu   It's just hard to share them. They're done individually.

Mark   Oh well.

Lulu   Well . . . hello.

Mark   Hello.

Lulu   We've got really into the little boxes with the whole thing in it. One each.

Robbie   Listen, listen, listen. You're looking so . . .

Lulu   Yes?

Robbie   Looks great, doesn't she?
Gonna be on TV, aren't you?

Mark   You've got a job?

Lulu   They're . . . considering it. It's just a / little . . .

Robbie   Just she says. Only. It's TV.

Mark   Great.

Robbie   You see, we're doing something? Aren't we?

Lulu   Yes.

Robbie   We're working. Providing.

Mark   So will I. Yes. I'll sort myself out and we'll be
OK.

Lulu   They're really not made for sharing. It's difficult.

Mark   It's OK. I'll go out.

Robbie   Back to Wayne?

Mark   No. Out. Find some food. Shopping.

Robbie   Don't just – don't stand there and judge us.

Mark   Cheeseburger. Some chocolate maybe.

Robbie   I want you to be part of this.

Mark   I've hurt you. I see that. But – please – just let
me . . . I've got to take this a step at a time, OK?

Exit **Mark**

Robbie   Cunt. Cunt. / Cunt.

Lulu   I know, I know.

Robbie   / Hate the cunt.

Lulu   That's it. Come on. / Come on.

Robbie   / Hate him now.

Lulu   Yes. Yes. Yes.

Robbie   I want him to suffer. I want.

Pause.

Lulu   Did you count / them?

Robbie   Oh. Yes. Yesyesyes.

Lulu   And was it? Three hundred exactly?

Robbie   Yes. Three hundred. Exactly.

Scene Four

A bedsit.

Gary *is sitting on a tatty armchair.* **Mark** *is standing.*

Gary   Course, any day now it'll be virtual. That's what they reckon.

Mark   I suppose that's right.

Gary   I'm planning on that. Looking to invest. The Net and the Web and that. You ever done that?

Mark   No. Never.

Gary   Couple of years time and we'll not even meet. We'll be like holograph things. We could look like whatever you wanted. And then we wouldn't want to meet cos we might not look like our holographs. You know what I mean? I think a lot about that kind of stuff, me.
See, I called you back. Don't do that for everyone.

Mark   Thank you.

Gary   Why d'ya pick me?

Mark   I liked your voice.

Gary   There must have been something special.

Mark   I just thought you had a nice voice.

Gary   How old did you think I was – on the lines?

Mark   I didn't think about it.

Gary   How old do you want me to be?

Mark   It doesn't matter.

Gary   Everybody's got an age they want you to be.

Mark   I'd like you to be yourself.

Gary   That's a new one.

Mark   I'd like to keep things straightforward.

Gary   You're in charge. Make yerself at home.
D'you want porn? I mean, it's mostly women and that but
it's something.
(*Indicating porn.*) She looks rough, doesn't she? Would you
shag her?

Mark   No. Let's leave the porn.

Gary   Or we could do some like . . . stuff, y'know.

Gary *pulls out a packet of cocaine.*

Gary   Share it with you.

Mark   No. Thank you.

Gary   It's thrown in. There's no extra / cost.

Mark   I don't want any.

Gary   It's quality. He don't give me rubbish.

Mark   Put it away.

Gary   I int gonna poison ya.

Mark   Put it away. Put the fucking stuff away.

Gary   All right, all right. Don't get knocky.

Mark   I don't want to see it. Please.

Gary   Look, it's all right stuff.

Pause.

Mark   I'm going.

Gary   You only just got here.

Mark   I can't be around people who use.

Gary   All right. Look. I'm putting it away.

Gary puts the packet in his trouser pocket.

See? All gone.
You stopping?

Mark   I'm sorry. I'm really sorry but I suppose I was
threatened by your actions. And my fear led me to an . . .
outburst. Which I now regret. It's just very important to
me. And I'd like you to acknowledge that.

Gary   You God Squad?

Mark   I'm sorry?

Gary   I had 'em before. We're at it and he kept going on
about Lamb of Jesus. Hit me. I give as good as I took.

Mark   No. I'm not God Squad.

Gary   Just got a thing about druggies?

Mark   I have a history of substance abuse.

Gary   You're a druggie?

Mark   I'm a recovering substance abuser.

Gary   You're not a druggie?

Mark   I used to be a druggie.

Gary   Got you.
So what you into?

Mark   You mean . . .

Gary   Sexwise.

Mark   Sexwise, I'd say I'm into the usual things.

Gary   So, you're looking for regular?

Mark   Pretty regular. The important thing for me right now, for my needs, is that this doesn't actually mean anything, you know?
Which is why I wanted something that was a transaction. Because I thought if I pay then it won't mean anything. Do you think that's right – in your experience?

Gary   Reckon.

Mark   Because this is a very important day for me. I'm sorry, I'm making you listen.

Gary   Everyone wants you to listen.

Mark   Right. Well. Today, you see, is my first day of a new life. I've been away to get better. Well, to acknowledge my needs anyway. And now I'm starting again and I suppose I wanted to experiment with you in terms of an interaction that was sexual but not personal, or at least not needy, OK?

A distant sound of coins clattering.

Gary   Downstairs. The arcade. Somebody's just had a win. You gotta know which ones to play otherwise all you get is tokens. I've a lucky streak me. Good sound, int it? Chinkchinkchink.

Mark   I suppose what I'd like, what I'd really like is to lick your arse.

Gary   That all?

Mark   Yes. That's all.

Gary   Right. We can settle up now.

Mark   How much do you want?

Gary   Hundred.

Mark   A hundred pounds? No, I'm sorry.

Gary   All right. If it's just licking, fifty.

Mark   Look, I can give you twenty.

Gary   Twenty. What d'you expect for twenty?

Mark   It's all I've got.
I've got to keep ten for the taxi.

Gary   You're taking the piss int ya?

Mark   Look, I'll walk. Thirty.
It's all I've got.

Gary   I should kick you out you know that? I shouldn't
be wasting my time with losers like you. Look at you.
Druggie with thirty quid. I'm in demand, me. I don't have
to be doing this.
There's a bloke, right? Rich bloke, big house. Wants me to
live with him.
So tell me: why should I let you lick my arse?

Mark   Why don't you think of him? You could lie there
and think of him.
Just a few minutes OK? Thirty quid.
Just get my tongue up, wriggle it about and you can think
of him.
This isn't a personal thing. It's a transaction, OK?

Gary *pulls down his trousers and underpants.*

Gary   I shouldn't be wasting my time with this.

Mark *starts to lick* **Gary**'s *arse.*

He's a big bloke. Cruel, like, but really, really he's kind.
Phones me on the lines and says: 'I really like the sound of
you. I want to look after you.'

Clatter of coins.

Listen to that. They're all winning tonight. So I'll probably
move in. Yeah, probably do it tomorrow.

Mark *pulls away. There's blood around his mouth.*

Mark   There's blood.

Pause.

You're bleeding.

Gary Didn't think that happened any more.

Mark That's . . . I'm going.

Gary Look. Thought I'd healed, OK? That's not suppose
to happen.
I'm not infected, OK?
Punter gave me a bottle somewhere. Rinse it out.

Mark I've got to go.

Mark *goes to take the money.*

Gary You can't take that.
Lick me arse, you said. Licked me arse, didn' ya?

Mark I'll leave you ten.

Gary Rinse your mouth out.
We agreed thirty.

Mark Twenty. I need ten for the taxi.

Gary Thirty – look, I need the money – please – I owe
him downstairs – can't live on tokens – give me the thirty.
You promised.

Mark Have the thirty.

Mark *gives* **Gary** *the thirty pounds.*

Gary Stay. Rinse it out. You'll feel better. It's
champagne.

Gary *exits.* **Mark** *sits.*

Scene Five

Pub.

Robbie *hands* **Lulu** *a drink.*

Robbie   After ten minutes, I thought I'd got the wrong name. Checked the name. And then I thought: maybe it's the right name but the wrong pub. Because there could be two pubs with the same name. But probably not on the same street. So I checked. And there wasn't. The same name on this street. But then I thought there could be other streets with the same street name. So I looked it up, borrowed the book from this bloke and looked it – listen. Did you know? There's blood.

Lulu   On me?

Robbie   On you. You've got blood on your face.

Lulu   I thought so. Get it off.

Robbie   Why's that then?

Lulu   Please I want it off.

Robbie   Is that your blood?

Lulu (*pawing at her face*)   Where is it?

Robbie (*indicates forehead*)   Just – yeah – that's it.

Lulu   Is it all gone? Everything?

Robbie   Yes. It's all gone.
Was that your blood?

Lulu   No. It must have splashed me.

Robbie   Whose blood is it?

Lulu   Why does it have to be like this?

Robbie   I knew something was up.

Lulu   I mean what kind of planet is this when you can't even buy a bar of chocolate?

Robbie   I think that's why I worried so much.

Lulu   And afterwards of course you feel so guilty. Like you could have done something.

Robbie   They attacked you?

Lulu   Not me. The Seven-Eleven.
Walking past and I think: I'd like a bar of chocolate. So I
go in but I can't decide which one. There's so much choice.
Too much. Which I think they do deliberately.
I'm only partly aware – and really why should I be any
more aware? – that an argument is forming at the counter.
A bloke. Dirty, pissy sort of –

Robbie   Wino?

Lulu   Probably. Wino sort of bloke is having a go at this
girl, young –

Robbie   Student?

Lulu   Yes. Student girl behind the counter. Wino is
raising his voice to student.
There's a couple of us in there. Me – chocolate. Somebody
else – TV guides. (Because now of course they've made the
choice on TV guides so fucking difficult as well.)
And wino's shouting: 'You've given me twenty. I asked for
a packet of ten and you've given me twenty.'
And I didn't see anything. Like the blade or anything. But
I suppose he must have hit her artery. Because there was
blood everywhere.

Robbie   Shit.

Lulu   And he's stabbing away and me and TV guide we
both just walked out of there and carried on walking.
Different directions.
And I can't help thinking: why did we do that?

Robbie   Look. It's done now.

Lulu   I could have stayed.
Am I clean?

Robbie   All gone.

Lulu   I could have intervened. Stopped him.
It's all off?

Robbie   Yes.

Lulu   Somebody could have fought him.

Robbie   No. They just go for you too.

Lulu   Or – I dunno – maybe reasoned with him.

Robbie   It's not TV.

Lulu   You never know. He might have seen reason.

Robbie   Like, 'Put down the knife, Mikey, just put down the knife.'

Lulu   It's like it's not really happening there – the same time, the same place as you. You're here. And it's there. And you just watch.
I'm going back.

Robbie   What for?

Lulu   Who called an ambulance? She could be lying there.

Robbie   No. There must have been someone.

Lulu   Or I could give a description.

Robbie   Did you see his face?

Lulu   No. No, I didn't.

Robbie   He's a wino. How they going to find a wino out there?

Lulu   I don't know.

Robbie . Look, they'll have a video. There's always like a security camera. They'll have his face.

Lulu . And I've still got. You see I took.

Lulu *produces the chocolate bar from her pocket.*

I took the bar of chocolate. She's being attacked and I picked this up and just for a moment I thought: I can take this and there's nobody to stop me.
Why did I do that? What am I?

Pause.

Robbie They must be used to it. Work nights in a shop like that, what do they expect?
You go home.

Lulu I can't.

Robbie You've had a shock. You need to rest.

Lulu We've got to do this.

Robbie I know.

Lulu Can't put it off any longer.

Robbie You're in no fit state. You've gotta sleep.

Lulu I don't want to sleep. I want to get on with this.

Robbie I'll do it.

Lulu We've got to do it together.

Robbie Think I can't manage? I can cope.

Lulu Of course you can.

Robbie I want to do it.

Lulu Out there on your own?

Robbie It's only selling. I can sell. Go home. Go to bed.

Lulu You're right. I am tired.

Robbie Then sleep.

Lulu They'll have me on the video. With the chocolate.

Robbie They'll be after him. Not you.

Lulu Suppose.
It's all here.

Lulu *gives* **Robbie** *a bum-bag.*

Robbie Right then.

Lulu Look there's just one rule, OK? That's what they reckon. If you're dealing. There's just rule number one. Which is: he who sells shall not use.

Robbie   Yeah. Makes sense doesn't it?

Lulu   Right. So just don't . . .

Robbie   Course not. Rule number one. I'm a big boy. Love you.

Lulu   Yeah. Love you too.
Do you think I look great?

Robbie   In the right light. And a fair wind.

Lulu   And a couple of E?

Robbie   . . . I better go.

Exit **Robbie**.
Lulu *looks at the chocolate bar for a beat. Then eats it very quickly.*

Scene Six

Bedsit.

Gary *hands* **Mark** *the bottle of champagne.*

Mark   I'm gonna go now.

Gary   Horrible, int it? Little kid with his arse bleeding.

Mark   Sorry. I just need to go.

Gary   Arse like a sore.

Mark   It's not that.

Gary   Thought I'd healed.

Mark   Yes, yes. Sure.

Gary   Comes into my room after *News at Ten*.

Mark   No, don't. Please.

Gary   Always after *News at Ten*. Tried to fight him off but I think he gets off on that.

Mark   Sure, sure, I understand.

Gary   I started to bleed.

Mark   No.

Gary   But I thought . . . now . . . I . . . got . . . away.

Mark   FUCKING SHUT UP, OK? KEEP YOUR
FUCKING MOUTH SHUT!

Gary   Sound like him.

Mark   Listen. I want you to understand because. I have
this personality you see? Part of me that gets addicted.
I have a tendency to define myself purely in terms of my
relationship to others. I have no definition of myself you
see. So I attach myself to others as a means of avoidance,
of avoiding knowing the self. Which is actually potentially
very destructive. For me – destructive for me. I don't know
if you're following this but you see if I don't stop myself
I repeat the patterns. Get attached to people, to these
emotions, then I'm back to where I started. Which is why,
though it may seem uncaring, I'm going to have to go.
You're gonna be OK?
I'm sorry, it's just –

Gary *cries.*

Mark   Hey. Hey. Hey.

Mark *makes a decision. He takes* **Gary** *in his arms.*

Mark   Come on. No. Come on. Please. It's OK.
Everything will be OK.
You don't have to say anything.

Gary   I want a dad. I want someone to look after me. I
want someone so strong that when he holds me in his arms
the world can't get to me. And I want him to fuck me, not
like that, not like him. Really fuck me. And yeah, it'll hurt.
But a good hurt. I never felt it but I know when I feel it
I've found him. Do you understand?

Mark   I think so.

Gary   Does everyone feel like that?

Mark   No.

Gary   What do you want?

Mark   I don't know yet.

Gary   You must want something. Everybody's got something.

Mark   So many years everything I've felt has been . . . chemically induced. I mean, everything you feel, you wonder: maybe it's just the coffee, you know, or the fags, or the, the . . . ozone.

Gary   The smack.

Mark   Yes. The smack, the Nutra-sweet.

Gary   The microwaves.

Mark   The cathode rays.

Gary   The mad cow. Moooooo.

Mark   Right. I mean are there are any feelings left, you know?

The coins clatter.

I want to find out, want to know if there are any feelings left.

Scene Seven

Accident and Emergency waiting room.

Robbie *sits bruised and bleeding.* **Lulu** *is holding a bottle of TCP.*

Lulu   I asked the Sister. She said I could.

It'll sting a bit. But with blood. It might get infected. Like gangrene.

Lulu *applies the TCP to* **Robbie**'s *face*.

Lulu   Keep still. Don't want to end up with, like, one eye, mmm?
Looks good actually.

Robbie   Yeah.

Lulu   Yes, suits you. Makes you look – well . . . tough.

Robbie   Good.

Lulu   I could go for you.

Lulu *strokes* **Robbie**'s *face*.

Robbie   Careful.

Lulu   Okay.

Robbie   Don't have to stop.

Lulu   Okay.

Robbie   Just easy, all right?

Lulu   Right.

Lulu *gently kisses the wounds*.

Robbie   Not gonna make it better.

Lulu   I know that.

Robbie   Never believed that did you? Let me kiss it better.

Lulu   No. I mean it.

Robbie   I know.

Lulu   Some people, a bruise, a wound, doesn't suit them.

Robbie   No.

Lulu   But you – it fits. It belongs.

Lulu *slips her hand into* **Robbie**'s *trousers and starts to play with his genitals.*

Lulu   Is that good?

Robbie   Yeah.

Lulu   That's it. Come on. That's it.
Tell me about them.

Robbie   Who?

Lulu   The men. Attackers.

Robbie   Them.

Lulu   The attackers. Muggers.

Robbie   Well –

Lulu   Sort of describe what they did. Like a story.

Robbie   No.

Lulu   I want to know.

Robbie   It's nothing.

Lulu   I don't want to just imagine.

Robbie   It wasn't like that.

Lulu   Come on then.

Robbie   Look.

Lulu   What was it like?

Pause.

Robbie   There was only one.

Lulu   Yes.

Robbie   Yeah.

Lulu   Didn't you say gang?

Robbie   No.
Just this one bloke.

Lulu   A knife?

Robbie   No.

Lulu   Oh.
So. He pinned you down?

Robbie   No.

Lulu   Got the money.

Robbie   I didn't – there wasn't any money, all right?
I never took any money.

Lulu   You never / sold?

Robbie   No.

Lulu   So before you even got there this man. With his
knife.

Robbie   / There wasn't a knife.

Lulu   Attacks and gets the E.

Robbie   No. I got there. I was there with the E.

Lulu   So?

Robbie   So.

Pause.

Lulu   You've lost it. (*His erection.*)

Robbie   Yeah.

Lulu   Gone limp on me.

Robbie   Yeah.

Lulu   Why's that then?

Pause.

Robbie   I was there. I was all ready. I was ready to deal.

Lulu   Right.

Robbie   There's a few other dealers. Stood around the dance-floor. I take up my position. I'm ready.
And this bloke comes up to me. Really, really nice looking. And he says, 'You selling?' Yeah, I say. Fifteen quid a go. And the way he looks at me, I know he fancies me, you know?
And he reaches in his pocket and – oh shit. So stupid.

Lulu   It was the knife, yes?

Robbie   There wasn't a knife.

Lulu   Gun?

Robbie   He. Look. He reaches in his pocket and says: 'Shit I left my money in my other jeans. Oh shit, now how am I gonna have a good time, now how am I gonna enjoy myself?'

Lulu   Right. Yes.
Go on.

Robbie   And he looked so . . . I felt sorry for him, all right?
But then he says: 'How about this? How about you give me the E? Give me the E now, then later, at the end, you can come back to mine and we can get the money from my jeans.'

Lulu   Right, so he was luring you. Luring you back to his / place

Robbie   No.

Lulu   Get you back to his so that he could pull the gun / or whatever.

Robbie   No.

Lulu   And get the Es off you.

Robbie   No, it didn't happen. That's not it.

Lulu   No?

Robbie   No.

So I said yes. It's a deal. And I gave him the E and he
takes it and I watch him and he's dancing and he's
sweating and smiling and he looks – well – beautiful and
just really, really happy.

Lulu   How many?

Robbie   What?

Lulu   You broke the first rule – yes? Yes?

Robbie   Yes.

Lulu   How many?

Robbie   I was out there on my own.

Lulu   How many?

Robbie   Three. Maybe four.

Lulu   Shit. I told you. Rule number one.

Robbie   I know.
But then, a few minutes later. A bloke. Even better, yes,
even better looking than the last bloke. And he says: 'Look
you gave my mate some E and I was wondering, I get paid
at the end of the week and if I give you my phone number
will you give me a couple of E?'

Lulu   You didn't?

Robbie   Yes.

Lulu   Fuck.

Robbie   And I felt good, I felt amazing, from just giving
you see?

Lulu   No, no I don't.

Robbie   But imagine. Imagine you're there, imagine how
it feels.

Lulu   No.

Robbie   And then – it sort of rolled. It flew.

Lulu   You prick. Three hundred.

Robbie   Until there's these guys, they're asking and I'm giving and everyone's dancing and smiling.

Lulu   Three hundred E. / Silly prick.

Robbie   Listen, listen to me. / This is what I felt.

Lulu   I don't want to know. / You gave away three hundred.

Robbie   / It's important.

Lulu   No. Stupid. Fucking. / Cunt.

Robbie   Just listen for a moment OK?
Listen this is the important bit. If you'd felt . . . I felt.
I was looking down on this planet. Spaceman over this
earth. And I see this kid in Rwanda. And this granny in
Kiev. And this president in Bogota or . . . South America.
And I see the suffering. And the wars. And the grab, grab,
grab.
And I think: Fuck money. Fuck it. Fuck selling. Fuck
buying. Fuck the bitching world and let's be . . . beautiful.
Beautiful. And happy. You see?
You see?
But now you see, but then I've only got two left and this
bloke comes up and says: 'You the bloke giving out the E?'
I give him the two but he says 'What two? Two. Two's not
going to do shit for me. You gotta have more.' And he
starts to hit, he starts to punch me.

Lulu   Wanker. Fucking fucker arsehole. Fuck.

She hits **Robbie** *in time with the following:*

Thought you were (*Hit.*) attacked.
Thought you were (*Hit.*) mugged.
Thought it was (*Hit.*) taken.
Should have been a (*Hit.*) knife.
You look like shit now. Look like you might get (*Throws the
bottle of TCP into* **Robbie**'s *eyes.*) gangrene.

Exit **Lulu**.

Robbie   Nurse. Nurse.

Scene Eight

Bedsit.

Mark *and* **Gary**.

Gary   I knew it wasn't right. I went to the council.
And I said to her, 'Look, it's simple: he's fucking me. Once,
twice, three times a week he comes into my room. He's a
big man. He holds me down and he fucks me.'
'How long?' she says. 'About two years,' I say. I say, 'He
moved in, then six months later it starts.' I told her and
she says 'Does he use a condom?'

Mark   Yeah?

Gary   Yeah. I mean, 'Does he use a condom?'
When it's like that he's not gonna use a condom is he? Just
spit. All he uses is a bit of spit.

Mark   On his – ?

Gary   Spit on his dick.

Mark   Of course.

Gary   And then she / says –

Mark   / And you –

Gary   The next thing / she says –

Mark   Does he / spit –

Gary   I told her that and / she says –

Mark   Does he spit up you?

Gary   Listen. I tell her he's fucking me – without a
condom – and she says to me – you know what she says?

Mark   No. No, I don't.

Gary   'I think I've got a leaflet. Would you like to give him a leaflet?'

Mark   Fuck.

Gary   Yeah. Give him a leaflet.

Mark   Well –

Gary   No, I don't want a leaflet. I mean, what good is a fucking leaflet? He can't even read a fucking leaflet, you know.

Mark   Yes.

Gary   And there's this look – like . . . panic in her eyes and she says: 'What do you want me to do?'

Mark   Right.

Gary   'Tell me what you want me to do.'

Mark   And you said – ?

Gary   Well, I don't know. Inject him with something, put him away, cut something off. Do something. And I'm – I've got this anger, right? This great big fucking anger – here in front of my eyes. I mean, I fucking hate her now right?

Mark   So did you / attack?

Gary   I go: Fuck. Fuck.

Mark   Maybe a knife or something?

Gary   I'm just shouting it over and over. FUCK.

Mark   You attacked / her?

Gary   So. In this little box, little white box room, I stand on the table and I shout: 'It's not difficult this is it? It's easy this. He's my stepdad. Listen, he's my stepdad and he's fucking me.'
And I walk away and I get on the coach and I come down here and I'm never going back. Gonna find something else.

Because there's this bloke. Looking out for me. He'll come and collect me. Takes me to his house. He's keeping a room for me. A special room.

Mark Look, this person that you're looking for . . .

Gary Yeah?

Mark Well, it's not me.

Gary Of course not.

Mark No.

Gary Fuck, you didn't think . . . ? No. It's not meant to be you. Never meant to be you.

Mark Good.

Gary You and me we're looking for different things right?

Mark Right.

Gary Mates?

Mark Mates.

Gary So – mate – do you wanna stay?

Mark I don't know.

Gary Stay if you like. Room on the floor. Someone waiting up for you?

Mark Not exactly.

Gary You stay long as you want.

Mark Thank you.

Gary Stay around and you can keep yourself busy. Give us a hand. Taking messages, cleaning up. Chucking out the mental ones.
Tell you what, you hang around long enough, we can . . .

Gary *pulls out a holdall from behind the chair. He unzips the bag. It is full of fifty-pence pieces. He catches up handfuls and lets them cascade through his fingers.*

See? I'm a winner, me. Every time. And I don't let them
give me tokens.
I can pay for what I want.
Stick around, you and me could go shopping yeah?

Mark   I don't know.

Gary   It's only shopping.

Mark   All right then. Yeah. Let's go shopping.

Gary   Listen to that. Best sound in the world.

They both listen to the coins as they run through **Gary**'s *fingers.*

Scene Nine

Flat.

Brian, **Lulu** *and* **Robbie. Brian** *inserts a video.*

Brian   Watch. I want you to see this.

*They watch a video of a schoolboy playing a cello. They sit for some
time in silence.* **Brian** *starts to weep.*

Brian   Sorry. Sorry.

Lulu   Would you like a – something to wipe?

Brian   Silly. Me a grown man.

Lulu   Maybe a handkerchief?

Brian   No. No.

*He pulls himself together. They sit and watch again for some time,
but eventually he starts to weep again.*

Brian   Oh, God. I'm so – I'm really sorry.

Lulu   No, no.

Brian   It's just the beauty, you see? The beauty of it.

Lulu   Of course.

Brian   Like a memory, you know, memory of what we've lost.

Pause.

Lulu   Are you sure you don't want − ?

Brian   Well −

Lulu   It's no problem.

Brian   Well then.

Lulu (*to* **Robbie**)   Could you − ?

Robbie   No problem.

Robbie *exits. They continue to watch the video.* **Robbie** *enters again with a toilet roll, takes it over to* **Brian**.

Brian   What's this?

Robbie   It's for your − you know to wipe your −

Brian   I asked you what it is.

Robbie   Well.

Brian   So, tell me what it is. What is in your hand?

Robbie   Well −

Lulu   Darling.

Brian   Yes?

Robbie   Toilet paper.

Brian   Toilet paper exactly. Toilet paper. Which belongs in the −

Robbie   Toilet.

Brian   Exactly.

Lulu   Darling I didn't mean . . . that.

Brian   And we use it to − ?

Robbie   Well, wipe your arse.

Brian   Exactly. Wipe your arse. While I – what is this?
(*Wipes eye.*)

Lulu   I didn't mean toilet paper.

Robbie   It's a – like a tear.

Brian   It is a tear. Little drop of pure emotion. Which
requires a – ?

Robbie   Well, a hanky.

Brian   Handkerchief.

Robbie   Handkerchief.

Lulu   Of course, I meant a handkerchief.

Robbie   Yes.

Lulu   So could you bring a – ?

Brian   This is disrupting you know that?

Lulu   Sorry.

Brian   This isn't – we're not in a supermarket or, or a
disco. Music like this, you listen.

Lulu   Yes.

Again they all settle down to watch the video. After a while, **Brian**
starts to cry, but even more so this time.

Brian   Oh, God. Oh, God. God.

Lulu   He's very good.

Brian   You feel it like – like something you knew.
Something so beautiful that you've lost but you'd forgotten
that you've lost it. Then you hear this.

Lulu   You must be very proud.

Brian   Hear this and know what you've . . . l-l-l-o-o-ost.

Brian *starts to sob heavily.*

Lulu   Look, I think I've got one.

Robbie   A handkerchief?

Lulu   Yes. A handkerchief. In the bedroom.

Robbie   Shall I fetch it?

Lulu   Well – yes. Yes, I think you should.

Exit **Robbie.**

Brian   Because once it was paradise, you see? And you could hear it – heaven sung to you, right? There was heaven singing in your ears. But we sinned, went and sinned, you see, and God took it away, took away music until we forgot we even heard it but sometimes you get a sort of glimpse – music or a poem – and it reminds you of what is was like before all the sin.

Enter **Robbie,** *offers hankerchief to* **Brian.**

Brian   Is it clean?

Robbie   Yes.

Brian   Again. Is it clean?

Robbie   Yes.

Brian   Again. Is it clean?

Robbie   Yes.

Brian   Look me in the eyes. Straight in the eyes. Yes?

Robbie (*does so*)   Yes.

Brian   And again – is it clean?

Robbie   No.

Brian   Then why did you offer it to me?

Robbie   Well –

Brian   Dirty handkerchief. Offer a dirty handkerchief.

Lulu   Darling –

Brian   Handkerchief for your nose.

Brian *punches* **Robbie**. *He slumps to the floor.*

Robbie   I'm – sorry.

Lulu   Take it away.

Robbie   Yes. Sorry.

Robbie *crawls out as they settle down in front of the video.*

Brian   His teacher says – and it's a religious school, very
religious school – his teacher says 'It's a gift from God.'
And I think that's right. Think that must be right because
it can't be from us. Doesn't come from me and his mother.
I mean, where does it come from if it's not from God, eh?
Kid like that, nice kid – his father's son, but nothing special
– picks up a bit of wood and string and, well, grown men
cry.

Robbie *enters.* **Brian** *removes a pristine hankerchief from his top
pocket and carefully wipes his eyes.*

Brian (*to* **Robbie**)   See. You don't wipe your eyes with
something that's been up your nose, all right?

Robbie   Yes. Sorry.

They continue to watch the video.

Brian   Think of the life he's gonna have eh? Think of
that.

Pause.

Brian   Because he doesn't know it now of course. But
when he's older, when he knows about sin, about all this,
then he's gonna thank God he's got this isn't he? This little
bit of purity.

Lulu   It is amazing isn't it?

Robbie   Yeah. Yeah. Really – amazing.

Lulu   That it just looks so effortless.

Brian   But there is effort.

Lulu   Of course.

Brian   Behind it all is effort.

Lulu   Have to practise all the time don't they?

Brian   His effort – yes.

Lulu   For like – hours a day.

Brian   His efforts – of course – but also my efforts.

Lulu   Of course.

Brian   Because, at the end of the day, at the final reckoning, behind beauty, behind God, behind paradise, peel them away and what is there? (*To* **Robbie**.) Son, I'm asking you.

Robbie   Well –

Brian   Come on son.

Robbie   Well –

Brian   Answer the question.

Robbie   Well, a father.

Brian   Sorry?

Robbie   You can't have them without a sort of a dad.

Brian   No. No. Think again. Try again.

Robbie   Well, I –

Brian   Think.

Robbie   No.

Brian   No, no. That's not good enough – no. Behind beauty, behind God, behind paradise –

Robbie   Money.

Brian   Yes. Good. Excellent. Money. Takes a few knocks, doesn't it, son?

Yeah.

But we get it knocked into us, don't we, eh? Learn the rules.

Money. There's boarding fees and the uniforms, the gear, the music, skiing.

Which is why I run such a tight ship you see? Which is why I have to keep the cash-flow flowing you see? Which is why I can't let people FUCK. ME. AROUND. You understand?

Lulu   Of course.

Brian   Which is why, right now, I feel sad and sort of angry. Yes?

Lulu   Yes.

Brian   I don't like mistakes. I don't like my mistakes. And now you tell me I've made a mistake. And so I hate myself. Inside. My soul.

We have a problem. Three thousand pounds of a problem. But what is the solution?

*They sit for a moment and contemplate this. Finally, **Brian** gets up, ejects the video, puts it back into its case.*

I have a gang, group of men, you know that?

Pause.

Who break legs.

Pause.

This could be a stalemate. Unless one of us concedes. But would you concede? Could you concede anything?

Lulu   No.

Brian   So what you're saying is – you're asking me to concede?

Lulu   Yes.

Brian   You think I should concede?

Long pause.

Seven days. To make the money.

Lulu Thank you.

Brian You understand? Son? Crackcrackrack.

Robbie Yes. Make the money. Yes.

Pause.

Brian Look at us. There is so much fear, so much wanting. But we're all searching.

Exit **Brian.**

Lulu Pillowbiter. Fudgepacker. Shitstabber.
Boys grow up you know and stop playing with each other's willies. Men and women make the future. Normal people who have kind tidy sex when they want it. And boys? Boys just fuck each other.
Seven days. The suffering is going to be handed out. And I shouldn't be part of that. But it'll be both of us. And that's not justice. Is it?

Robbie We'll be all right.

Lulu Yes? Yes?

Robbie We'll make the money. I know how to make the money.

Scene Ten

Changing room at Harvey Nichols. **Mark** *is trying on an expensive designer suit.*

Gary (*off*) How's it going?

Mark Yeah. Good.

Gary Do you want the other size?

Mark   No. This is great.

Gary   All right then.

Mark   Have a look, if you like.

Enter **Gary**. *He is transformed: top-to-toe designer gear and carrying bundles of expensive shopping bags.*

Gary   Oh yes.

Mark   Like it?

Gary   Oh yeah. It's you. Suits you. Do you want it?

Mark   I don't know.

Gary   If you like it, you have it.

Mark   I mean, it's not like I'm even gonna wear it.

Gary   You don't know that. You're starting over.

Mark   I do like it.

Gary   Could be anything. New life, new gear. It makes sense. Go on.

Mark   You sure you can / afford . . . ?

Gary   Hey. None of that.

Mark   All right, then. Yes.

Gary   Good, and now we'll . . .

He holds out a handful of credit cards as if they were playing cards.

Pick a card, any card.

Mark *picks a card. Reads the name on it.*

Mark   P. Harmsden.

Gary   You remember? Last night. Poppers. Kept on hitting himself.

Mark   Ah. P. Harmsden.

Gary   Right then. Get it off and then we're eating out.
My treat.

Mark   Why don't you . . . wait outside?

Gary   I'm not bothered.

Mark   Have a look round. I'll only be a few minutes.

Gary   Too late now. I've seen it.

Mark   Seen the . . . ?

Gary   Seen the hard-on.

Mark   Ah yes. The hard-on.

Gary   Must be aching by now. Up all day.
Is it the shopping does that?

Mark   I don't know.

Gary   You gotta thing about shopping?

Mark   I don't think so.

Gary   Or is it cos of me?

Mark   I'm not sure.

Gary   How old do you think I am?

Mark   I don't know.

Gary   When you met me – what did you think?

Mark   I don't . . . sort of sixteen, seventeen.

Gary   Right.
What's going on in your head?
I mean, I can see what's going on in your pants but what's
in there?
Tell me.

Mark   Nothing. Look. It's just a physical thing you know?

Gary   For me? Physical thing for me?

Mark   Yes.

Gary   Thinking about me?

Mark   It's not thinking. Just wanting.

Gary   You want me? You can have me.
Why don't you say what you want?
Do you want to kiss me?

Mark   Yes.

Gary   Go on then.

Mark   I'm frightened.
Listen if we do . . . anything, it's got to mean nothing, you understand?

Gary   Course.

Mark   If I feel like it's starting to mean something then I'll stop.

Gary   You can kiss me, like a gentle kiss. Me mum, she's got a nice kiss. Kiss me like you're me mum.

Mark *kisses* **Gary**.

Gary   How was that?

Mark   Yes. That was all right.

Gary   Bit more?

Mark   Bit more.

Mark *kisses* **Gary** *again. This time it becomes more sexual. Eventually,* **Mark** *pulls away.*

Mark   No. I don't want to do this.

Gary   I knew it. You've fallen for me.

Mark   Fuck. I really thought I'd broken this, you know?

Gary   Do you love me?

Mark   I really wanted to break the pattern.

Gary   Is that what it is? Love?

Mark I don't know . . . just something.

Gary I didn't feel anything.
Which means . . . gives me the power doesn't it?
Hey, don't worry. I'm not gonna abuse it.

Mark I think we should . . . I think it's time I went back to my own place OK?

Gary Come with you if you like.

Mark No, you get on with your life and . . .

Gary Show us where you live. Mates. Friends. You said.

They kiss again.

It's not true about me mum. I don't let her kiss me. She's a slag.
You gonna fuck me?

Mark I don't know.

Gary Reckon you will.
(*Caresses* **Mark***'s crotch.*) All this. For me.
You want something that bad, you better do it.

Mark Yes. Come here.

Gary *undoes* **Mark***'s trousers, kneels in front of him.* **Gary** *waves upwards.*

Mark ?

Gary Security camera. We gonna stay here?

Mark What do you want to do?

Gary I'm not bothered.

Mark All right. We'll stay here.

Gary *starts to suck* **Mark***'s cock.*
Pulls away.

Gary Fourteen.

Mark What?

Gary   You got it wrong. I'm fourteen.

Gary *carries on sucking cock.*

Scene Eleven

Flat.

Robbie *and* **Lulu** *sit. The 'phone is ringing. There are two recently cooked ready meals in front of them.*

Robbie   Well?

Lulu   Yes?

Robbie   Are you going to answer it?

Lulu   No.

Robbie   Come on. Answer it.

Lulu   It's your turn.

Robbie   It's not.

Lulu   So you answer it.

Robbie   I did the last one.

Lulu   I did the last one. You answer it because it's your turn.

Robbie   I'm not answering it.

Lulu   Why is it always me?
If you're not prepared when it's your turn.

Robbie   Your turn.

The 'phone stops ringing.

Lulu   There now. You see?
That was another wasted opportunity wasn't it?
And why aren't you eating?

Robbie   Don't want to. I'm not hungry.

Lulu   Look. I'm offering you food. I don't have to but I want to.

Robbie   No. Couldn't keep it down.

Lulu   And why is that?

Robbie   I'm sick.

Lulu   Oh yes? As in ill?

Robbie   No. Sick of this. Money. Dirty talk. Day after day. I don't want to be doing this. This isn't living. I want to be free.

Lulu   And why? Why are we living like this?

Pause.

Robbie   All right. I'll try.

They start eating. The 'phone starts to ring.
They both stop and look at it.
Eventually **Lulu** *goes to answer it.*

Lulu   Hello?
Yes. Yes. All right. If you give me the card number. Yes. Yes. And the expiry date? There's always an exp – . Uh, uh, yeah.
OK. Well, it's Roman times. OK. It's BC. And I'm in one of those old – I'm in the Parthenon OK? Well maybe it's Greek – I don't know – but – look – it's somewhere really – yes – ancient. OK?
And I'm watching the athletes. That's right. The gladiators. And there's this one gladiat – yes, it's you. I'm watching you. Now this guy, this senator comes up to me. Fat senator and he says: 'See the one with the javelin? Well, he's my slave. He's my slave but I'm pissed off with him. I hate him so much now that unless I can sell him today I think I'll probably kill him. I want to kill him today.'
Yes. He hates you. Why? Why does he hate you? Yes, that's right.

'Do you want to buy him?' says the fat senator.
'I'll swap you,' I say. 'Six chickens.'
Yes. Six. Because that's all your worth.
So we do the deal and I take you away. Take you back to
the hold of my ship and I manac – yes, I put you in irons.
And in the darkness you hear the voice of this little old
man.

She gestures to **Robbie**. *He turns away.*

Voice of a little old man and he says –

Lulu *holds out the 'phone to* **Robbie**.
Pause.

Robbie (*reluctantly*) So, are you his new slave?

Lulu Yes. Yes. Old man, I am the new slave.

Robbie Beware. Beware. Do you know what the last
slave died of?

Lulu *takes back the 'phone.*

Lulu Yes. Yes. Close. Close now.
'What old man?' you ask. 'How did the slave die?'
But before he can answer, the door into the hold is open
and down I come. I'm drunk. I've got my sword in my
hand.
Yes. Yes. Almost there.
Good. So you've – ? Good. Good.
Well. I don't know.
I don't usually –
Not as a rule. No.
I see. Yes. Yes. And how much would you be prepared
to – ?
One hundred. I see. Yes.

Robbie What's he saying?

Lulu Maybe if we doubled that.
(*To* **Robbie**.) Wants to meet.

Robbie No.

Lulu Well that sounds all right. Yes. I think we could manage something for that.

Robbie Stop it. Stop now.

Lulu And when would be convenient?

Robbie No.

Robbie *snatches the 'phone from* **Lulu**.

Lulu Give me that.

A brief tussle which **Robbie** *wins.*

Robbie (*into 'phone*) No. No she doesn't want to meet you. Nobody wants to meet you. Because it's a rule. You're a punter. Know your place, punter.

Lulu No. Give it to me.

Robbie Goodbye.

He hangs up.
Long pause.

Lulu I thought that now you'd got something in the real world, a job, then maybe you'd – what? – grow up? Yes, grow and maybe . . . mature.
Now. There are two days to go. So if someone is actually paying . . .

Robbie You used our story.
You told him the shopping story.

Lulu It was different. I changed it.

Robbie It was still the shopping story.

Lulu Well. Maybe that's what he wanted to hear.

Robbie You shouldn't have done that.

Lulu Two days to go and we tell them whatever they want to hear.
Now. Eat.

Robbie *starts to eat but soon pushes his away.*

Lulu   Don't stop.

Robbie   I'm not / eating that.

Lulu   You've only just started. Don't stop.

Robbie   I can't. It doesn't taste of anything.

Lulu   Of course it tastes of something.

Robbie   Then maybe it's me.

Lulu   Of course it's you.

Robbie   Yes. It's my fault. Fine. I don't want it.

Lulu   What's wrong with the − ? Look. / I'm eating. If I can.

Robbie   I don't want the food.

Lulu   And why? / What is so wrong that you can't eat it?

Robbie   I'm not eating.

Lulu   I mean, you've got the world here. You've got all the tastes in the world. You've got a fucking empire under cellophane. Look, China. India. Indonesia. I mean in the past you'd have to invade, you'd have to fucking occupy just to get one of these things and now, when they're sitting here in front of you, you're telling me you can't taste anything.

Robbie   Well, yes. Yes, I am. There's no taste. This stuff tastes of nothing.

Lulu   Eat it. Eat it. Eat it.

Robbie   This stuff?

Lulu   Now. Eat it now.

Robbie   No. This? This is shit. This? I wouldn't feed a fucking paraplegic / paraplegic with cancer this shit.

Lulu Eat it.

She pushes **Robbie***'s face into the food.*

China. India. Indonesia. Eat it. All those starving babies.
Africa. Eat it for them. EAT IT.

Lulu *and* **Robbie** *start fighting, forcing food into each other's mouths.*
Enter **Mark** *and* **Gary**.

Mark   Hello.

Lulu *and* **Robbie** *stop, covered in food.*
Pause.

Robbie   Where have you – ?

Pause.

(*To* **Gary**.) He went out to get chocolate.

Gary   Yeah?

Robbie   Five days ago, chocolate or a cheeseburger from
the shop.
So what has brought you back?

Mark   Wanted to see where I lived. Didn't I?

Gary   Yeah.

Mark   Show you where I live.

Gary   Didn't say there'd be / other people.

Mark   Show you who I live with.

Robbie   And here we are. I'm Barney. This is Betty.
Pebbles is playing outside somewhere.

Pause.

Lulu   We're just . . . eating.

Gary   Is that really your name?

Lulu   Sitting down for a meal. It's actually very difficult
to share them actually, because they are specifically
designed as individual portions, but I can get an extra
plate. Plate. Knife. Whatever.

Gary   You're not called Betty, are you?

Mark   No no no. I don't think we're that hungry.

Robbie   We? We? Listen to that. We.

Mark   Well, I don't think we are.

Robbie   You on special offer?

Gary   You what?

Lulu   It all got a bit messy.

Robbie   Cheaper than a Twix?

Gary   He don't need to pay me.

Robbie   Really?

Gary   Some people, you give it away, don't you?

Mark   Gary, this is Lulu.

Lulu   Things got out of hand.

Robbie   He will do. He's got this thing. Has to make it a transaction.

Gary   Not with me.

Lulu   Let's sit down, shall we? Let's all sit. Yes?

They all sit.

Well, look at this mess. If you don't watch yourself, you just revert don't you? To the playground or the canteen and suddenly it's all food fights and mess.
So let's be adults. Not much but I think I can still . . . a portion. Anyone?

They sit in silence.

Robbie   So – you're special?

Gary   He thinks so.

Lulu   Actually you know I think there's probably enough for two.

Robbie   He said that? He told you that?

Mark   Come on now. Leave him alone.

Gary   Can look after meself.
Yes. He said that.

Robbie   Tell me.

Mark (*to* **Robbie**)   Leave him alone.

Gary   I want them to know.

Lulu   Somebody please eat.

Robbie   Come on.

Lulu   I'm really looking forward to pudding.

Robbie   Tell me what he said to you.

Gary   He said: I love you.

Mark   Hey come on, come on.

Gary   Yeah, yeah. I love you. I'd be lost without you.

Mark   It wasn't those words.

Robbie (*to* **Gary**)   You're lying. Fucking lying.

He leaps on **Gary** *and starts to strangle him.*

Gary   No. It's true. Please. 'S true. He loves me.

Mark   Leave him alone. Get off. Off.

Mark *attacks* **Robbie**, *who is attacking* **Gary**.
Lulu *tries to protect the ready meals, but they are crushed in the mêlée.*

Lulu   Stop it. Stop. Now.

Mark *succeeds in pulling* **Robbie** *off* **Gary**. *The fight subsides.*

Gary   Loony. You're a fucking headcase, you are.

Lulu   Come on, leave it, now leave it.

Gary   Fucking going for me.

Lulu   Ssssh . . . quiet . . . quiet.

Long pause.

Robbie   'I love you.'

Lulu   Forget it.

Robbie   That's what he said you said.
Didn't you?

Mark   I never said – because – look – I don't.

Exit **Mark**.

Lulu   Mess. Look at this. Why is everything such a mess?

Lulu *scrapes up as much food as she can on to the tray and exits.*
Robbie *and* **Gary** *regard each other in silence.*

Gary   He *does* loves me. He did say that.

Robbie   Did he do this – ask you to lick his balls while
he came?

Gary   Yeah. Have you . . . ?

Robbie   Too many times. I'm his boyfriend.

Gary   He doesn't do nothing for me, all right?

Robbie   No? Not your type?

Gary   He's too soft.

Pause.

Do you love him?

Robbie   Yes.

Pause.

Gary   It's all gentle with him. That's not what I'm
after. Just marking time. Got to find this bloke. I know he's
out there. Just got to find him.

Robbie   Someone who's not gentle?

Gary   Yeah, someone strong. Firm, you know.

Robbie   Yes.

Gary   You think he's cruel but really he's looking out for you. I'm going to be somewhere. I'll be dancing. Shopping. Whatever. And he'll fetch me. Take me away.
If I can just keep on looking.

Robbie   If he exists.

Gary   You what?

Robbie   If he really exists.

Gary   You saying I'm lying?

Robbie   I didn't say that.
I think . . . I think we all need stories, we make up stories so that we can get by.

Gary   This is for real, this is.

Robbie   And I think a long time ago there were big stories. Stories so big you could live your whole life in them. The Powerful Hands of the Gods and Fate. The Journey to Enlightenment. The March of Socialism. But they all died or the world grew up or grew senile or forgot them, so now we're all making up our own stories. Little stories. But we've each got one.

Gary   Yes.

Robbie   It's lonely. I understand. But you're not alone. I'm offering to help. A helping hand.
For a fee.

Gary   Yeah?

Robbie   Yeah. Pay me and you'll get what you want.

Gary   All right. A thousand. If I get what I want.

Robbie   Cash. It's got to be cash.

Gary   Course.

Robbie   You've got the money?

Gary   Yeah. I've got the money.

He tips open his bag. Silver coins flood out.

Scene Twelve

The flat.

Mark, Gary, Lulu *and* **Robbie.**

Mark   Why are we playing this?

Robbie   Because he wants to.

Mark   It's a stupid game.

Robbie   Your friend. Isn't that right?

Gary   Right.

Mark   Why do you want to play this?

Gary   In my head, I see this picture, all right?

Lulu   Yes.

Gary   Well, like a picture but like a story, you know?

Robbie   Yes?

Gary   A sort of story of pictures.

Lulu   A film.

Gary   Yeah, story like a film.

Robbie   With you?

Gary   Yes.

Lulu   You're in the film?

Gary   Yes.

Robbie   You're the hero – ?

Gary   Well –

Lulu   You're the protag – you are the central character of the film?

Gary   Sort of. Yeah.

Robbie   Right.

Gary   So there's this story, *film* and I –

Pause.

Robbie   What?

Gary   No. Look, I don't want to . . .

Lulu   You don't want to –

Gary   I thought I could, but I can't, all right? It's just saying it. Sorry.

Robbie   So – just wasting our time?

Gary   I'm sorry.

Robbie   We should have got the money first.

Mark   Which money?

Lulu   You're not going through with this?

Gary   I don't know.

Robbie   You should have paid upfront.

Mark   Some sort of a bet?

Gary   I'm paying after.

Mark   Paying for . . . ?

Robbie   Paying to play the game.

Lulu   So do you want to do this?

Pause.

Robbie   Pointless. Wasting our time. I mean, how old are you? What are you? Some kid wasting our time.

Gary   I'm not a kid.

Robbie You don't know what you want.

Gary I know what I want.

Lulu So . . . ?

Gary It's just . . . the words. It's describing it.

Mark All right. Come back to him.

Robbie Now, as I'm the judge –

Mark Do me. Ask me – truth or dare?

Robbie That's not fair. That's not in the rules, is it?

Mark But if he's not ready.

Robbie Right. A forfeit. Something I'd like you to . . . something by way of punishment.

Mark Just leave it, OK?

Gary Shit, I don't want to.

Robbie (*to* **Lulu**) What do you think would be a suitable punishment?

Mark (*to* **Gary**) It's all right. It's all right.

Gary Shit.

His tears are close to hysteria.

Mark I'll do it. We can come back to you.
Now – ask me a question.

Robbie No.

Mark Come on – ask me a question.

Lulu All right.

Robbie It's cheating.

Lulu I know. My question is . . . My question is: who is the most famous person you've ever fucked?

Mark The most famous person?

Lulu The most famous person.

Mark Well, OK then, OK.

Robbie If you're gonna . . . it's got to be the truth.

Mark Yeah, yeah.

Robbie Or it doesn't count.

Mark I know.

Lulu Come on. The most famous person.

Robbie No, because last time –

Lulu Come on.

Robbie No, because before.

Lulu Let him say it.

Robbie You made it up last time.

Mark I know, I know.

Robbie So, what I'm saying is –

Mark I know what you're saying.

Robbie I'm saying it's got to be true.

Mark Right.

Beat.

Robbie Right.

Beat.

Lulu Well, then –

Mark Well, then. I'm in Tramp, OK? Tramp or Annabel's, OK?

Robbie Which – ?

Mark I can't remember.

Robbie Look, you've got to –

Lulu   Go on.

Mark   Tramp or Annabel's or somewhere, OK?

Robbie   If you don't know where.

Mark   It doesn't matter where, OK?

Robbie   If it's true, then –

Mark   The place, the name doesn't matter.

Lulu   No. It doesn't matter.

Robbie   I think you should know –

Mark   What the fuck does it matter where?

Lulu   All right.

Mark   When what you said was who.

Lulu   Come on. Who? Who? Who?

Mark   Tramp or Annabel's or some place. Some place because the place is not of importance OK? Because the place doesn't matter. So I'm at this somewhere place –

Robbie   When?

Mark   Jesus.

Lulu   It doesn't matter.

Robbie   I want to know when.

Lulu   Come on, you're there and –

Robbie   I want to know when.

Mark   Some time. In the past.

Robbie   The last week past? The last year past? Your childhood past?

Lulu   The past past.

Mark   Well, I don't –

Robbie   Come on –

Lulu   Why?

Robbie   Veracity. For the /

Mark   / all right then, all right /

Robbie   / veracity of it.

Mark   '84. '85. About then. OK?

Robbie   OK.

Mark   So I'm in this place – which is maybe Tramp maybe not – and it's possibly nineteen eighty-five –

Robbie   That's all I wanted to know.

Mark   I'm having a good time.

Robbie   Meaning?

Mark   Meaning a good time. Meaning a time that is good.

Robbie   Meaning you've taken –

Mark   Meaning I'm having a time that is good.

Robbie   Because you've taken –

Mark   Not necessarily.

Robbie   But you had?

Mark   I don't know.

Robbie   Come on. '84. '85. You must have been on something.

Mark   Well, yes.

Robbie   Yes.

Mark   Probably yes.

Robbie   Because really, when can you say you're not –

Mark   What? Go on, what?

Robbie   When can you say you're not on something?

Mark   Now.

Robbie   Yeah?

Lulu   Come on. Come on.

Robbie   You're sure? Sure that you're not –

Mark   Yes.

Lulu   Let's – the story.

Mark   I'm fucking clean all right?

Lulu   Come on. '84. '85. Tramp. Annabel's.

Robbie   Yeah. Right.

Mark   I mean, what the fuck do I have to – ? I'm clean, OK?

Lulu   Please. I want to know who.

Mark   All right. Just don't – all right. Tramp. '84. I'm having a good time.

Robbie   You're tripping?

Mark   No. And I need a piss, yes?

Lulu   In the toilet?

Mark   Yes, a piss in the toilet.

Lulu   This is a toilet story.

Mark   So, I'm making my way to the toilet, right? And there's this woman, OK? This woman is, like, watching me.

Lulu   Who? Who? Who?

Mark   Of course, I should have known then. I should have known who she was.

Lulu   Who?

Mark   But, I mean, I am so –

Robbie   You're tripping.

Mark   No.

Robbie   You should have known who she was but you're tripping.

Mark   Look, I was not tripping.

Robbie   You didn't recognize this famous person because you were completely out of it.

Mark   Okay, okay, I was completely out of it.

Lulu   And you're on your way to the toilet.

Mark   Out of it. All I know is that this woman's eyes are like: give me your veiny bang stick, OK?

Lulu   Way with words.

Mark   So I'm pissing. Urinals. I'm pissing in the urinals and in the mirror I can see the door, OK? Well, OK. Pissing and the door opens. Door opens and it's her.

Lulu   So you're, what − in the ladies?

Robbie   Urinals in the ladies?

Mark   Nope.

Robbie   So this is the −

Mark   Urinals in the gents.

Robbie   So she's −

Mark   She's there in the gents, OK? Standing in the gents watching me piss, OK? And now, now we're in, like, bright − we're in fluorescent light, I see.

Lulu   Who? Who? Who?

Mark   Not yet.

Robbie   Why not?

Mark   Because I'm out of it, OK? As you say, I'm on something. I should know who, but I don't recognize her, OK?

Lulu   So then bright light and you see . . . ?

Mark   See what she's wearing. A uniform. She is wearing a police uniform.

Lulu   Fuck. Who? Who? Who?

Robbie   A man's uniform or – ?

Mark   WPC. The docs, the stockings, the jacket. The works. The hat. And she looks me in the eyes –

Gary   A woman?

Robbie   You're pissing?

Mark   Looks me in the eyes by way of the mirror, OK?

Robbie   OK, OK.

Gary   You did it with a woman?

Mark   She looks, she, she, she cruises me and then goes into one of the cubicles, but looking at me all the time, you know? Goes into one of the cubicles and leaves the door ajar. I want to race right in there you know? Get down to it but, like you do, I count to ten. Count to ten and then like coolly walk past. And as I walk past, I take a cool glance to my right, cool look into the cubicle, cubicle with the door ajar and – wow!

Lulu   Wow?

Mark   Wow! The skirt is up around the waist. The skirt is up and the knickers are off or maybe she never had knickers – who knows? – but the skirt is up and she is, like, displaying this beautiful, come-and-get-it snatch to die for, OK?

Gary   Said you didn't go for women.

Robbie   Facing / you?

Lulu   Who is it?

Mark   So I'm in there. I'm in and I kneel. I pay worship. My tongue is worshipping that pussy like it's God. And that's when she speaks. Speaks and I know who she is.

Lulu   Who?

Mark   She says 'Yuh. Yuh. Yuh, oh yuh.'

Lulu   No!

Robbie   What?

Gary   Is this a woman?

Lulu   No – it can't be.

Robbie   I told you.

Lulu   That is fucking unbelievable.

Robbie   Yes, yes it is.

Lulu   Diana?

Mark   Yup.

Lulu   Diana Diana?

Mark   I recognize the voice. Get a look at the face. Yes. It's her.

Robbie   Come on –

Mark   So a couple of minutes later, I'm there, I'm fucking Diana, it's pumpity-pump against the cistern.

Robbie   You can't believe this.

Mark   Pumpity-pump and the door, door to the cubicle starts to open.

Robbie   This is ridiculous.

Mark   I haven't locked the door, you see.

Robbie   We said the truth. It had to be the truth.

Mark   Rule number one. Always lock the door.

Robbie   No one believes this.

Mark   Door opens and another woman. Another policewoman like squeezes her way in. With red hair.

Robbie   I think you should stop.

Lulu   What – Fergie?

Robbie   Come on.

Mark   Fergie.

Lulu   Fucking hell.

Robbie   Do you believe this?

Lulu   Well –

Robbie   How can you believe this?

Mark   Fergie is like 'chocks away'. Fergie is right down to it. Fergie is ready to swallow anything, you know?

Robbie   Stop it. Stop.

Mark   So there's Fergie here. There's Di here. And I'm working away.

Robbie   SHUT UP! SHUT THE FUCK UP!

Pause.

Mark   What? What I thought you wanted to know . . .

Robbie   The truth.

Mark   Which is what . . .

Robbie   No.
(*To* **Lulu**.)   Do you believe him?
(*To* **Gary**.)   Do you?

Pause.

Rule number one. Never believe a junkie.

Pause.

Gary   Why didn't you tell me you'd done it with a woman?

Robbie (*to* **Gary**)   Back to you.

Gary   All right.

Robbie   It's your turn now.

Mark   You don't have to –

Gary   I want to.

Lulu   We'll help you.

Gary   Yeah?

Lulu   Help you to find the words.

Robbie   All right then. All right. Your story. Your film, yeah?

Gary   Yeah.

Robbie   I think I know what it is. I see. I understand.

Gary   Yeah?

Robbie   Yes. These pictures in your head.
So if I help – yes? If I can help you to describe the pictures, then –

Gary   Yes.

Robbie   All right. All right. There's you, yes, and you're. I see you . . . there's music, yes?

Gary   Music. Yes.

Robbie   Loud music. Dum dum dum. Like / techno.

Gary   Techno music. Yes.

Robbie   Techno music and you're moving like – you're dancing yes?

Gary   Yeah, dancing.

Robbie   Dancing on a dance-floor. Dance-floor in a club.

Gary   Yes. Yes. A club.

Robbie   What's the – ? I see – damp?

Gary   Sweat.

Robbie   Good. Yes. Sweat. It's . . .

Gary   Hot.

Robbie   Hot, so it's . . .

Gary   Summer.

Lulu   Good. Hot. Summer. Techno. Dance-floor.

Gary   Dancing and it's hot.

Robbie   You're dancing with this guy.

Gary   No. Not like that.

Robbie   Dancing by yourself but now . . .

Gary   There's a bloke.

Robbie   Bloke who's watching you.

Gary   I'm dancing.

Lulu   He's watching.

Gary   He's watching me.

Lulu   And you smile.

Gary   No smile.

Robbie   But you know, you think –

Gary   I think. I think I don't have a choice.

Lulu   No choice.

Gary   No control.

Robbie   No control.

Lulu   Because he's –

Robbie   I'm going to have you.

Mark   Come on leave –

Robbie   No.

Mark   This is – it's getting heavy.

Gary   No.

Robbie   We're getting to the truth.

Gary   I want to say it.

Lulu   Now there's another –

Robbie   A fat bloke.

Gary   A fat bloke?

Lulu   Bloke watching you is talking to a fat bloke.

Gary   Yeah, he's talking to the fat bloke. And he's saying?

Robbie   See that one dancing?

Lulu   See that one dancing?

Robbie   Yeah. Yeah. I see him.

Lulu   Well, he's mine. I own him.

Mark   Fuck's sake.

Lulu   I own him but I don't want him.

Gary   Don't want him. You . . .

Lulu   You know something.
He's trash and I hate him.

Robbie   Hate him.

Gary   Hate me.

Robbie   And the fat bloke says –

Lulu   Well, you wanna buy him?

Gary   Yes.

Robbie   And / I say.

Gary   You say.

Robbie   How much?

Lulu   Piece of trash like that. Well, let's say twenty. He's yours for twenty.

Robbie   So you see the money.

Gary   I see money. See you pay him.

Robbie *pulls twenty quid from his pocket and gives it to* **Lulu**.

Robbie   You've seen the trans . . .

Gary   Trans . . .

Robbie   Good.

Gary   Transaction. I've seen the transaction.

Robbie   Yes, and I come to . . .

Gary   To fetch me. You don't say anything. You say nothing. Just take me away.

Robbie   Good. Take you away.

Mark *stands up.*

Mark   All right, stop. Stop now. Because I think we've seen . . . I think we've got the truth now, haven't we?

Gary   I'm wearing a, there's like a . . . can't see . . .

Lulu   A blindfold? You want – ?

Gary   Blindfold. There's, like, a blindfold.

Lulu *produces a blindfold.*

Mark   No.

Lulu   Do you understand what I'm going to do to you?

Gary   Yes.

Lulu   You understand and do you want me to do this?

Gary   Yes.

Mark *pushes* **Lulu** *away and puts his arms around* **Gary.**

Mark   See? That's good, isn't it? You can choose this instead, you see. You must like that. That's nice, isn't it?

Gary   What are you doing?

Mark   Just holding you.

Gary   And you gonna fuck me?

Gary *pushes* **Mark** *away.*

Gary   What you doing to me? You're taking the piss, aren't you? I don't want this.

Mark   I'm just trying to show you. Because, I don't think that you have ever actually been loved.

Gary   It's not what I'm after. It's all gentle with you.

Mark   Because we can only comprehend that for which we have the vocabulary, you see, and if the world has offered us no practical definition of love / in practice.

Gary   What are you?

Mark   I can take care of you.

Gary   You're nobody. You're not what I want. I –

Mark   If you can just get out of this trap and be free.

Gary   I don't want you. Understand?
You're nothing.

Mark *retreats.*
Lulu *puts the blindfold on* **Gary***.*

Robbie   Blindfold you and –

Gary   Take me to –

Robbie   To my house –

Gary   To your house.

Lulu *and* **Robbie** *spin* **Gary** *around.*

Robbie   And you see the house. And you know it. Know you've seen it somewhere before.

Gary   Where have I seen it before?

Lulu   And now. Now a bare room.

Gary   I know who you are. You're . . . yes . . . you're my dad.

Robbie No. / No. I'm not.

Gary Yes, it's my dad's house.

Robbie I don't want to do this.

Lulu Darling.

Robbie *takes off the blindfold.*

Gary Why you stopping?

Lulu He wants to carry on.

Robbie I can't if he says that.

Gary I want to finish the story.

Robbie Just don't – I'm not your / dad, all right?

Lulu Well, all right.

Robbie I'm not your father.

Gary I want to, please. I want to carry on.

Robbie *replaces the blindfold.*

Gary Yes.

Robbie And now.

Gary You tie me.

Robbie Yes.

Gary You tie my hands.

Lulu *ties* **Gary**'s *hands.*

Lulu So – you're the new slave?

Robbie Yes. Yes, old woman. This is the new slave.

Lulu Beware. Beware. Do you know what the last slave died of?

Gary What? What old woman? What did the last slave die of?

Robbie Now.

Lulu   Sssssh. He's coming. The master is coming.
Sssssshhh.

Robbie   Handle. Handle on the door turning.

Silence. **Gary** *stands very still.* **Robbie** *slowly approaches him
from behind. Long pause –* **Robbie** *inches away from* **Gary**.

Gary   Go on.

Robbie   Yes?

Gary   Do it.

Robbie   It's what you want?

Gary   Yes.

Robbie   It's what you're paying for?

Gary   Yes.

Robbie *starts to undo* **Gary**'s *trousers.*

Robbie   Yes?

Gary   Yes.

Robbie *pulls down* **Gary**'s *trousers.*

Robbie   Pay me now.

Gary   I'll pay you after.

Robbie *spits on his hand. Slowly he works the spit up* **Gary**'s
arse.

Robbie   Now?

Gary   Do it now.

Mark   Look, I need to. I want to.

Mark *slowly comes toward* **Gary** *and* **Robbie**.

Lulu   You can't stop it now.

Mark   No.

Mark *kneels at* **Gary**'s *feet. Beat as he looks up.*

Then he starts searching in the pockets of **Gary***'s trousers, which are now round his ankles. Finally, he finds the little packet of cocaine. He pulls back and in an orderly fashion sets about taking the cocaine.* **Robbie** *spits on his hand. Slowly he works the spit up* **Gary***'s arse.*

Robbie   Now.

Robbie *unzips his fly. Works spit onto his penis. He penetrates* **Gary**.
He starts to fuck him.
Silence. **Robbie** *continues to fuck* **Gary**. **Mark** *starts to sob quietly.*

Lulu   Is that good? Do you like that?

Gary   Yes.

More silent fucking.

Robbie (*to* **Mark**)   Do you want him?

Mark   I . . .

Robbie   Do you know what he is? Trash. Trash and I hate him. Want him? You can have him. Want him and he's all yours.

Mark   Yes.

Robbie *pulls away.* **Mark** *goes through the same routine – spitting and penetrating* **Gary**. *He fucks him viciously.*

Mark   Fuck you. Fuck you.

Lulu   Does it hurt? Is it hurting you?

Gary   Are you – ?

Mark   Don't say it.

Gary   Are you my dad?

Mark   No.

Gary   Yes. You're my dad.

Mark   I told you – no.

Mark *hits* **Gary**.
Then, he pulls away from **Gary**.

Gary   See. See. I know who you are. I never met you but when it feels like that I know that I've found you.

Mark   No.

Mark *hits* **Gary** *repeatedly*

I'm. Not. Your. Dad.

Lulu   Leave him. Leave him now.

She pulls **Mark** *away from* **Gary**.

Mark   I don't want to be anyone's dad.

Lulu   Nearly there. Nearly . . . yes . . . so don't stop now.

Robbie   You wanna carry on?

Gary   Yes.

Robbie *gets into position to continue fucking* **Gary**.

Gary   Wait. This bit. It isn't right.

Robbie   No?

Gary   Because – look – this bit. In my story. My story doesn't end like this. He doesn't just fuck me.

Robbie   No?

Gary   No. Because in the story he's always got something. It depends, changes. He gets me in the room, ties me up. But he doesn't just wanna fuck me does he?
Cos it's not him, it's not his dick, it's a knife. He fucks me with a knife. So . . .

Pause.

Gotta have something.
Everybody's got something. The kitchen. Or, or a screwdriver. Or something.

Lulu   No.

Gary   Got to be fucking something. That's how the story ends.

Robbie *pulls off* **Gary***'s blindfold.*

Robbie   No. I'm not gonna do that.

Gary   You're not gonna finish like this?

Robbie   I can't do that.

Lulu   You'll bleed.

Gary   Yeah.

Lulu   You could die.

Gary   No. I'll be OK. Promise.

Robbie   It'll kill you.

Gary   It's what I want.

Lulu   Go home now.

Gary   Just do it. Just fucking do it.
You're losers – you're fucking losers you know that?

Robbie   Yeah.

Gary   Listen, right. When someone's paying, someone wants something and they're paying, then you do it. Nothing right. Nothing wrong. It's a deal. So you do it.

Robbie *unties* **Gary***'s hands*

Gary   I thought you were for real.

Robbie   I know.

Gary   Pretending isn't it? Just a story.

Robbie   Yes.

Mark (*to* **Robbie** *and* **Lulu**)   Please leave us now.

Lulu   We need his money. We want to survive.

Mark   I know. If you leave us alone. Yes?

Exit **Robbie** *and* **Lulu**.

Gary   I want you to do it. Come on. You can do it.
I've been looking. Looking and I can't find him.
You knew that, didn't you? Because he's not out there.
No. Because he's been here all the time.
I've got this unhappiness. This big sadness swelling like it's
gonna burst. And it's hurting me.
I'm sick and I'm never going to be well again.
I want it over. And there's only one ending.

Mark   I understand.

Gary   He hasn't got a face in the story. He's in my head
– waiting – but. I want to put a face to him. Your face.
Do it. Do it and I'll say 'I love you'.

Scene Thirteen

The flat.

Brian, Lulu *and* **Robbie** *sit watching the video of the boy
playing the cello. They all have ready meals on their laps.* **Brian**
has a holdall. **Mark** *sits apart from them.*

Brian   You know, life is hard. On this planet. There is so
much fear, so much wanting. I can tell you this because I
feel it. Yes, like you I have felt this too. We work, we
struggle. And we find ourselves asking: what is this for? Is
there meaning? I know you've . . . I can see this question
in your eyes. You ask yourself these questions. Right now –
yes?

Robbie   Yes.

Brian   And you – what is there to guide me on my
lonely journey?
Yes?

Lulu   Yes.

Brian We need something. A guide. A talisman. A set of rules. A compass to steer us through this everlasting night. Our youth is spent searching for this guide until we . . . some give up. Some say there is nothing. There is chaos. We are born into chaos, we exist in chaos, and finally we are released from chaos. But this is . . . no. This is too painful. This is too awful to contemplate. This we deny. Am I right?

Robbie Yes.

Brian Yes. I have a rung a bell. Good, good. Bells are rung.
Chaos or . . . order. Meaning. Something that gives us meaning.

Pause.

My dad once said to me. My dad said it to me and now I'm going to say it to you. One day my dad says to me: 'Son, what are the first few words in the Bible?'

Robbie In the beginning.

Brian No.

Robbie Yes. In the beginning.

Brian I'm telling you no.

Robbie That's what it says. In the beginning.

Brian No, son. I'm telling you no. And you listen to me when I'm telling you no, all right?

Robbie All right.

Brian 'Tell me son,' says my dad, 'what are the first few words in the Bible?' 'I don't know dad,' I say, 'what are the first few words in the Bible?'
And he looks at me, he looks me in the eye and he says: 'Son, the first few words in the Bible are . . . get the money first.' Get. The Money. First.

Pause.

It's not perfect, I don't deny it. We haven't reached
perfection. But it's the closest we've come to meaning.
Civilization is money. Money is civilization. And civilization
– how did we get here? By war, by struggle, kill or be
killed. And money – it's the same thing, you understand?
The getting is cruel, is hard, but the having is civilization.
Then we are civilized. Say it. Say it with me. Money is . . .

Pause.

SAY IT. Money is . . .

Lulu *and* **Robbie**   Civilization.

Brian   Yes. Yes. I'm teaching. You're learning. Money is
civilization. And civilization is . . . SAY IT. Don't get
frightened now. And civilization is . . .

Lulu *and* **Robbie**   Money.

Brian *offers them the holdall.*

Brian   Here. Take it.

Lulu   You . . . ?

Brian   I want you to take it.

Lulu   It's all there.

Brian   Yes.

Lulu   Look – if you want to count it. Three thousand.

Brian   Take it from me when I tell you to take it.

Lulu *takes the bag.*

Brian   Good. Good. You see? Do you understand? I am
returning the money. You see?

Lulu   I . . . yes.

Brian   And now – you have a question. Ask me the
question. Please. Ask the question?

Lulu   Why?

Brian   If you formulate the question . . .

Lulu   Why didn't you take the money? Why did you give us back the money?

Brian   And now I can answer you. I answer: because you have learnt. The lesson has been learnt you see. You understand this (*Indicates the money.*) and you are civilized. And so – I return it. I give it to you.

Lulu   Thank you.

Brian *gets up, moves to video player. He ejects the video of his son. Takes another video from his pocket. Places it in the machine. Pushes play.*

Lulu (*TV*)   One day we'll know what all this was for, all this suffering. There'll be no more mysteries, but until then we have to carry on living . . . / we must work, that's all we can do. I'm leaving by myself tomorrow, I'll teach in a school, and devote my whole life to people who need it. It's autumn now, it'll soon be winter, and there'll be snow everywhere, but I'll be working . . . yes, working.

Brian   It's the future isn't it? Shopping. Television. It's time to move on. These chemicals. Supplies aren't the best. So a kid dies. And then it's headlines and press conferences. And you watch the dad, you watch a grown man cry and you think: time to move out of chemicals.

Brian *pauses the tape.*

And now you've proved yourselves, I'd like you to join us. Both of you.

He moves to the exit.

Think about it. The future. We won't see it, of course. That purity. But they will. The kids. My boy. Generations to come. They'll know it. And what we've got to do is make the money. Just keep on making money. For them. Our second favourite bit was the end. Because by then he's got married. And he's got a kid of his own. Right at the end he stands alone. He's on a rock and he looks up at the

night, he looks up at the stars and he says: 'Father.
Everything is all right Father. I remembered. The Cycle of
Being.' (Words to that effect.)
You ought to see it. You'd like it.

Exit **Brian**. **Mark** *comes forward.*

Mark   It's three thousand A.D. Or something. It's the
future. The Earth has died. Died or we killed it. The
ozone, the bombs, a meteorite. It doesn't matter. But
humanity has survived. A few of us . . . jumped ship. And
on we go.
So, it's three thousand and blahdeblah and I'm standing in
the market, some sort of bazaar. A little satellite circling
Uranus. Market day. And I'm looking at this mutant. Some
of them, the radiation it's made them so ugly, twisted. But
this one. Wow. It's made him . . . he's tanned and blond
and there's pecs and his dick . . . I mean his dick is three
foot long.
This fat sort of ape-thing comes up to me and says . . .
'See the mute with the three foot dick?'
Yeah. I see him.
'Well, he's mine and I own him. I own him but I hate him.
If I don't sell him today I'm gonna kill him.'
So . . . a deal is struck, a transaction, I take my mutant
home and I get him home and I say:
'I'm freeing you. I'm setting you free. You can go now.'
And he starts to cry. I think it's gratitude. I mean he
should be grateful but it's . . .
He says – well, he telepathizes into my mind – he doesn't
speak our language – he tells me:
'I'll die. Please. I can't . . . I've been a slave all my life. I
don't know how to . . . I can't feed myself. How will I find
somewhere to live? I've never had a thought of my own.
I'll be dead in a week.'
And I say: 'That's a risk I'm prepared to take.'

Robbie   Thirty-six inches and no shag?

Mark   That's right.

Lulu   I like that ending.

Robbie   It's not bad.

Mark   It's the best I can do.

Robbie   Hungry now? I want you to try some. (*Of the ready meal.*)

Robbie *feeds* **Mark** *with a fork.*

Robbie   Nice?

Mark   Mmmmm.

Robbie   Now give him some of yours.

Lulu   Do you want some?

Lulu *feeds* **Mark**.

Is that good?

Mark   Delicious.

Lulu   Bit more?

Mark   Why not?

Lulu *feeds him.*

Robbie   My turn.

Robbie *feeds* **Mark**.

Mark, **Robbie** and **Lulu** *take it in turns to feed each other as the lights fade to black.*

Methuen Modern Plays

include work by

Jean Anouilh
John Arden
Margaretta D'Arcy
Peter Barnes
Sebastian Barry
Brendan Behan
Edward Bond
Bertolt Brecht
Howard Brenton
Simon Burke
Jim Cartwright
Caryl Churchill
Noël Coward
Sarah Daniels
Nick Dear
Shelagh Delaney
David Edgar
Dario Fo
Michael Frayn
John Godber
Paul Godfrey
John Guare
Peter Handke
Jonathan Harvey
Iain Heggie
Declan Hughes
Terry Johnson
Barrie Keeffe
Stephen Lowe
Doug Lucie

John McGrath
David Mamet
Patrick Marber
Arthur Miller
Mtwa, Ngema & Simon
Tom Murphy
Phyllis Nagy
Peter Nichols
Joseph O'Connor
Joe Orton
Louise Page
Joe Penhall
Luigi Pirandello
Stephen Poliakoff
Franca Rame
Philip Ridley
Reginald Rose
David Rudkin
Willy Russell
Jean-Paul Sartre
Sam Shepard
Wole Soyinka
C. P. Taylor
Theatre de Complicite
Theatre Workshop
Sue Townsend
Judy Upton
Timberlake Wertenbaker
Victoria Wood

Methuen World Classics

Aeschylus (two volumes)
Jean Anouilh
John Arden (two volumes)
Arden & D'Arcy
Aristophanes (two volumes)
Aristophanes & Menander
Brendan Behan
Aphra Behn
Edward Bond (four volumes)
Bertolt Brecht
    (five volumes)
Büchner
Bulgakov
Calderón
Anton Chekhov
Noël Coward (five volumes)
Sarah Daniels (two volumes)
Eduardo De Filippo
David Edgar (three volumes)
Euripides (three volumes)
Dario Fo (two volumes)
Michael Frayn (two volumes)
Max Frisch
Gorky
Harley Granville Barker
    (two volumes)
Henrik Ibsen (six volumes)
Terry Johnson
Lorca (three volumes)

Marivaux
Mustapha Matura
David Mercer (two volumes)
Arthur Miller
    (five volumes)
Anthony Minghella
Molière
Tom Murphy
    (three volumes)
Musset
Peter Nichols (two volumes)
Clifford Odets
Joe Orton
Louise Page
A. W. Pinero
Luigi Pirandello
Stephen Poliakoff
    (two volumes)
Terence Rattigan
Ntozake Shange
Sophocles (two volumes)
Wole Soyinka
David Storey (two volumes)
August Strindberg
    (three volumes)
J. M. Synge
Ramón del Valle-Inclán
Frank Wedekind
Oscar Wilde

Methuen Student Editions

John Arden	*Serjeant Musgrave's Dance*
Alan Ayckbourn	*Confusions*
Aphra Behn	*The Rover*
Edward Bond	*Lear*
Bertolt Brecht	*The Caucasian Chalk Circle*
	Life of Galileo
	Mother Courage and her Children
Anton Chekhov	*The Cherry Orchard*
Caryl Churchill	*Top Girls*
Shelagh Delaney	*A Taste of Honey*
John Galsworthy	*Strife*
Robert Holman	*Across Oka*
Henrik Ibsen	*A Doll's House*
Charlotte Keatley	*My Mother Said I Never Should*
John Marston	*The Malcontent*
Willy Russell	*Blood Brothers*
August Strindberg	*The Father*
J. M. Synge	*The Playboy of the Western World*
Oscar Wilde	*The Importance of Being Earnest*
Tennessee Williams	*A Streetcar Named Desire*
Timberlake Wertenbaker	*Our Country's Good*

new and forthcoming titles in the Methuen Film series

Beautiful Thing
Jonathan Harvey

The Crucible
Arthur Miller

Twelfth Night
Trevor Nunn after Shakespeare

The Krays
Philip Ridley

The Reflecting Skin & The Passion of Darkly Noon
Philip Ridley

The English Patient
Anthony Minghella